CAMBRIDGE MUSIC HANDBOOKS

Beethoven: *Missa solemnis*

CAMBRIDGE MUSIC HANDBOOKS

GENERAL EDITOR Julian Rushton

Cambridge Music Handbooks provide accessible introductions to major musical works, written by the most informed commentators in the field.

With the concert-goer, performer and student in mind, the books present essential information on the historical and musical context, the composition, and the performance and reception history of each work, or group of works, as well as critical discussion of the music.

Other published titles

Bach: Mass in B Minor   JOHN BUTT
Berg: Violin Concerto   ANTHONY POPLE
Handel: *Messiah*   DONALD BURROWS
Haydn: *The Creation*   NICHOLAS TEMPERLEY
Mahler: Symphony No. 3   PETER FRANKLIN

Beethoven: *Missa solemnis*

William Drabkin
Senior Lecturer in Music
University of Southampton

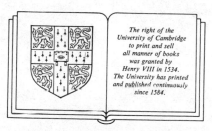

Cambridge University Press
Cambridge
New York   Port Chester
Melbourne   Sydney

Published by the Press Syndicate of the University of Cambridge
The Pitt Building, Trumpington Street, Cambridge CB2 1RP
40 West 20th Street, New York, NY 10011–4211, USA
10 Stamford Road, Oakleigh, Melbourne 3166, Australia

© Cambridge University Press 1991

First published 1991

Printed in Great Britain at the University Press, Cambridge

British Library cataloguing in publication data
Drabkin, William
Beethoven: Missa Solemnis – (Cambridge music handbooks)
1. Masses
I. Title
782.3232092
ISBN 0 521 37229 1

Library of Congress cataloguing in publication data
Drabkin, William
Beethoven: Missa solemnis / William Drabkin
p.   cm. – (Cambridge music handbooks)
ISBN 0 521 37229 1. – ISBN 0 521 37831 (pbk).
1. Beethoven, Ludwig van, 1770–1817. Missa solemnis
I. Title. II. Series
ML410.B42D8   1991
782.32′32–dc20   91–11383   CIP   MN

ISBN 0 521 372291 hardback
ISBN 0 521 378311 paperback

for Andrea

Contents

Contents

Tables

Preface

The idea of writing a handbook on the *Missa solemnis* was suggested to me in 1988 by the general editor of this series. At the time, I was working at a project on the sketches and autograph score for the Agnus Dei; I welcomed the opportunity to take a step back from my research to look at the Mass as a whole. Reading the substantial literature on the work helped me to place it in its historical context, and to decide what new avenues of investigation might be most fruitfully explored.

As most writings on the Mass are concerned with explaining it as Beethoven's major contribution to religious music, the work has been perceived largely as a religious and personal statement by the composer. Two writers have been quick to observe that little has actually been said about how the work holds together, section by section, phrase by phrase. In 1936 Walter Riezler expressed his astonishment that the Mass had not been subjected to a full-scale analytical study. 'Even Schenker has written nothing about it' (Riezler 1938: 187), he remarked, just a year after Schenker's death and more than a generation before voice-leading analysis took root in the soil of musical academia. Almost a quarter of a century later, in 1959, the German sociologist and music critic Theodor Adorno, in a polemical critique of the Mass, admitted that, despite much historical and philosophical rumination, there was as yet no objective study of the music that related its 'innermost compositional cells' to its structure (Adorno 1964: 160).

And so the challenge of writing about the *Missa solemnis* was, for me, the challenge of writing about how it is put together. What I offer here will, I hope, be of help to those who would like to understand it as a musical composition. For this reason, the largest portion of the text is devoted to an explanation of how the Mass works musically. The riches of works like the Mass cannot, of course, be exhausted by a single analytical excavation; what is offered here may be thought of as at most a blueprint for investigation, and at least – I hope – as an encouragement for further study of its structure and the details which make that structure come to life.

I do not cling to the (once fashionable) view that everything of significance in a musical work can be wrested from its score: the *Missa solemnis* has proved fertile territory for the study of Beethoven's art in relation to his life, to the history of music and to posterity. I hope that the initial chapters of this book will encourage further reading about Beethoven and the Mass, just as I would like the remaining ones to stimulate further thinking.

Though this study is largely about the music, limitations of space have necessitated my keeping musical illustrations to a minimum. Where I believe that my arguments can be verified in the score itself, I refer the reader to the relevant passages.

No special abbreviations have been used in the text, except for the familiar 'op.' (opus number) and 'WoO' (Werk ohne Opuszahl, work without opus number) taken from the standard thematic catalogue of Beethoven's work (Kinsky and Halm 1955; supplement in Dorfmüller 1978).

I refer frequently to the masses of Joseph Haydn, many of which are known by more than one name. For purposes of identification, I use a mixture of German, Latin and English names which, I believe, are current in English-speaking countries:

Number*	Key	Name used in this book	Other names
HXII:6,	G major	*Nikolaimesse*	Missa Sancti Nicolai; 6/4–Takt–Messe
HXII:7,	B♭ major	Little Organ Mass	Missa St^i Johannis de Deo; Kleine Orgelmesse
HXII:8,	C major	*Mariazellermesse*	Missa Cellensis
HXII:9,	C major	*Missa in tempore belli*	Mass in Time of War; Paukenmesse
HXII:10,	B♭ major	*Heiligmesse*	Missa Sancti Bernardi von Offida
HXII:11,	D minor	'Nelson' Mass	Imperial Mass; *Missa in angustiis*
HXII:12,	B♭ major	*Theresienmesse*	
HXII:13,	B♭ major	*Schöpfungsmesse*	'Creation' Mass
HXII:14,	B♭ major	*Harmoniemesse*	

* in the standard Haydn thematic catalogue, by Antony van Hoboken, vol. 2 (Mainz, 1971).

The musical settings of the five sections of the Mass Ordinary are described throughout as 'movements'. This is not to imply that a mass is no more than a symphony for voices and orchestra; calling them 'movements', however, enables me to use the word 'section' for a large portion (for example, the first 'Kyrie'), and 'subsection' for a smaller unit (for example, 'Consubstantialem Patrem', 'Qui propter nos homines'). Movements are capitalized in the text; sections and subsections are identified by their incipits surrounded by single quotation marks, except when Beethoven gives them a specific title. Thus the fourth movement, the Sanctus, is divided into an opening 'Sanctus' followed by the 'Pleni', the first 'Osanna', the Praeludium and the Benedictus. To avoid confusion, I call the last movement the Agnus Dei, its two sections the 'Agnus' and the 'Dona nobis pacem' (or 'Dona', for short).

Pitches are identified by the standard Helmholtz system, using super-scripts rather than primes. Thus c ... b, c^1 (=middle C) ... b^1, c^2 ... b^2, and so on. Pitch-classes, which I generally use for bass notes, are designated by capital letters (D = any D, and so forth).

In tables and music examples, major keys are designated by capital letters, minor keys by small letters. Secondary (or applied) harmonic functions are followed by a diagonal slash. Thus, for example:

Bb   the key of B flat major
V/IV the dominant of the subdominant ('V of IV')
V/g   the dominant of G minor

I am grateful to the librarians and archivists at the Beethovenarchiv in Bonn, and at the music divisions of the Staatsbibliothek Preußischer Kulturbesitz in Berlin and the Bibliothèque Nationale in Paris for per-mission to examine their Beethoven manuscripts. I owe a special debt of thanks to the staff of the Deutsche Staatsbibliothek in Berlin for granting me repeated access to pocket sketch-leaves for the Mass which have proved particularly resistant to transcription.

Critical perspectives

What Walter Riezler once called 'Beethoven's least approachable work', one that had 'been ignored by the commentators' (1938: 187), has in fact attracted a good deal of attention since it was published in early spring 1827, within days of the composer's death. Indeed it is difficult to imagine how the musical world could avoid coming to terms with it. The *Missa solemnis* is the largest and longest non-stage work written by a composer who, before he began it, had already shattered the dimensional barriers of the symphony, the string quartet and the sonata. It also took him far longer to write than any other work, and its composition makes up a substantial part of his musical life. Its position in Beethoven's *œuvre* as the largest sacred work, and the only one dating from his last decade, makes it a music–historical document of inestimable value.

The *Missa solemnis* as religious experience

Though biographers and critics have been unable to ignore the *Missa solemnis*, their writings have, perhaps unsurprisingly, emphasized the work's monumental qualities rather than focussing on the details of the musical experience. For most early commentators, Beethoven's second setting of the Mass Ordinary offered an opportunity to catch up on the composer's relationship to the divinity. It is well known that Beethoven, though born and brought up a Catholic, was not a regular church-goer. His revulsion against the existing social order which expected ordinary mortals – great artists not excepted – to defer to higher authorities, was reflected in a disdain of all ritual for its own sake. His musical legacy reflects this antipathy towards ceremony, comprising very little in the way of sacred music; and both *Christus am Ölberge* (The Mount of Olives), a relatively brief oratorio of 1803, and an earlier setting of the Mass, in C (1807), were composed in haste to meet tight deadlines. Despite the valiant efforts of a few champions, neither work has won general acclaim, and they are rarely considered to increase our understanding of Beethoven's musical development. Indeed, the fact that both works fall within the so-called 'heroic period' (and are roughly contemporary with the 'Eroica' and Fifth Symphonies respectively) makes their artistic failure all the more disappointing.

Seen in this light, the *Missa solemnis* is usually made to bear the full weight of Beethoven's musical expression of religious beliefs.[1] It has been viewed as marking a turning-point, comparable to the position of the 'Eroica' Symphony in 1803–4. In writing the 'Eroica' Beethoven had, by his own account, 'seized Fate by the throat' and was coming to terms with the reality by devoting himself to his art in the noblest way; it is with the *Missa solemnis* – not with *Christus* or the Mass in C – that he finally acknowledges the need to come to terms with God. The idea of a spiritual crisis around 1819, paralleling the personal–artistic crisis of 1802–3 – allowing us to divide Beethoven's *œuvre*, once again, into three creative periods – was proposed by Paul Bekker, an influential Berlin music critic of the first half of the twentieth century, whose Beethoven biography ran to over forty editions:

Beethoven's new material was the poetry of transcendental idealism. He abandons such symbols from the visible world as he had used in the *Eroica* and succeeding works, and turns towards the invisible, the divine ... the *Mass* became the second great turning-point of his art, as the *Eroica* had been the first. The third symphony embodies the 'poetic idea' to which Beethoven was groping in preceding works; the *Mass* presents the same idea, transfigured and spiritualised. Freedom, personal, social and ethical, is consecrated and raised to heights where every activity, even of an apparently earthly kind, is flooded with unearthly light.   (Bekker 1925: 270)

If a musical work embodies the spirituality of its composer, then it may be appropriate to regard it as the vessel of that spirituality, much as a church is seen to contain the collective spirituality of its congregation. For Adolf Bernhard Marx, whose life-and-works study of Beethoven is among the earliest to consider the work in detail, the *Missa solemnis*, while not actually being the musical representation of a great cathedral, is nevertheless inseparable from it. The following account of the beginning of the Credo is typical of his style:

All [performing forces] work with their full power so that the sound reverberates violently about the pillars of the cathedral and reaches up to strike the vaulting.
(Marx 1863: ii, 246)

For Marx, the musical image of the cathedral is made more vivid by the sound of the organ, not because the organ has any special role in the *Missa solemnis*, but rather because Beethoven uses the orchestra to simulate the effect of the instrument, for example in the 'Gratias' of the Gloria and the Praeludium linking the 'Osanna' to the Benedictus (1863: ii, 246, 251). For Bekker, the spacious opening of the Kyrie 'evokes the image of a huge cathedral' (1912: 382). More recently, Wilfrid Mellers had a similar idea in mind when he gave this movement the subtitle 'the Invisible Church' (1985: 291).

The *Missa solemnis* and music history

Another way in which writers sought to comprehend the immensity of the *Missa solemnis* was by relating it to major works in the repertory. It was commonplace, for instance, to regard Bach's B minor Mass and Beethoven's Mass in D as the two greatest settings of the Mass Ordinary, even allowing for the fact that they are organized along entirely different lines and were composed (in Bach's case, assembled) by quite different means (Butt 1991).

Even more frequent are comparisons with Handel's *Messiah*, held in Beethoven's time to be the greatest large-scale sacred work (the B minor Mass was not published until 1818, and was little known in Vienna). Most writers acknowledge a general kinship between Handel's choral writing and Beethoven's (the formal fugues are longer, and other fugal textures occur more frequently here than in the earlier Mass in C), and more specific reverberations of *Messiah* in the exuberant 'Gloria in excelsis Deo'. Even if the latter creates a Handelian impression mainly by featuring the trumpets in the second octave above middle C, where they are capable of playing a scale (and hence a melody), this in itself marks a significant departure from the conventional use of trumpets in Classical sacred music. Some writers trace a Handelian influence beyond the sections in D major and the choral fugues. Martin Cooper, for instance, maintains that the *Grave* which concludes the Credo's closing fugue displays 'full Handelian panoply'; more specifically, he suggests that the opening of the Agnus Dei, in B minor, is a 'clear reminiscence' of the bass aria 'The people who walked in darkness', and that the Benedictus may have been inspired by the *Sinfonia pastorale*, or 'Pifa' (Cooper 1970: 265–6).[2] And the majority of commentators believe that the fugato in the 'Dona nobis pacem' (bars 216ff.) is a deliberate quotation from the 'Hallelujah Chorus', or at least an unconscious reference to it. (This point will be discussed at greater length in chapter 8.)

A second way of linking the *Missa solemnis* to other works which have gained immortality is to regard it as a companion piece to Beethoven's next large compositional project, the Ninth Symphony. The first to dub this the 'sister work' of the Mass was the Augsburg *Kapellmeister* Wilhelm Weber. He found the spiritual and musical relations to the Mass in the choral finale of the Ninth so intense that, for the second edition of his monograph on the Mass (1908), he felt compelled to include a chapter on the Ninth as an appendix (1908: 146–55). Weber was also the first to discover a 'direct reference' to the Mass in the choral finale of the Ninth (1908: 68–9); more recently, William Kinderman discovered not merely isolated references but an entire 'network of referential sonorities' linking the Credo and Benedictus of the Mass to the chorale finale of the symphony (1985: 115).

One further constellation is provided by closing fugues in Bb from Beethoven's late years: the 'Hammerklavier' Sonata (1818), the Credo of the *Missa solemnis*, and the original finale of the String Quartet op.130 (1825, later published as a separate work under the title *Große Fuge*). Bekker, who was the first to suggest this grouping, did not subject the fugues – all, it turns out, from works dedicated to Archduke Rudolph of Austria – to a rigorous comparative analysis; but his view, that they are Beethoven's 'three most exalted and metaphysical works' (1925: 274), has been supported by other writers. Walter Riezler contrasted the closing fugues of the Gloria and Credo by regarding the music of the latter as 'furthest removed from worldly things' (1938: 193); Denis McCaldin saw in its closing moments the image of 'man's spirit leaving the earth and ascending to heaven' (1971: 406); and Cooper and Mellers in their different ways that the end of the Credo creates an other-worldly, distancing effect (Cooper 1970: 258; Mellers 1985: 334–5).

The *Missa solemnis* in the history of sacred music

A different link with tradition is suggested by Warren Kirkendale, in his informed account of the antecedents of the *Missa solemnis* (1970). Instead of siding with the common view of Beethoven's setting as a highly personal one, the product of a composer of great sophistication and a human being of naïve philosophical understanding and religious faith, Kirkendale viewed the work as the direct continuation of an approach to sacred music which sought to perpetuate musical convention and symbolism from as far back as the Renaissance. This 'rhetorical tradition' could help explain, for instance, the festive opening of the Kyrie, the modal 'Et incarnatus', the

4

trombone ritornelli in the first part of the Sanctus, and the exaggerated highlighting of certain words (for example, 'omnipotens' in the Gloria, 'judicare' in the Credo). The extent to which Beethoven consciously incorporated these elements into his Mass must remain conjectural: the evidence that he studied extensively sacred music of earlier ages, and the works of the ancient theorists, rests on a handful of remarks in the conversation books and letters. It is easy to overinterpret this evidence, yet Kirkendale's contribution is a valuable reminder to us that, whatever our own perception of Beethoven's antecedents may be, Beethoven's perception of them was certainly different.

In a parallel vein, Carl Dahlhaus suggested that Beethoven's second Mass might well have been deliberately written against the background of an essay on Church music by the writer and composer E. T. A. Hoffmann (Dahlhaus 1987: 237). Dahlhaus suspected that Beethoven had read Hoffmann's 'Alte und neue Kirchenmusik', which appeared in the *Allgemeine musikalische Zeitung* in 1814, since Hoffmann was well known for reviews lauding works from Beethoven's middle period (these include a long piece on the Mass in C). 'Alte und neue Kirchenmusik' can, in fact, be read as an expansion of the argument put forward in the review of the Mass in C, that sacred music had been in steady decline since the baroque period and had reached a nadir around the early nineteenth century (Hoffmann 1920: 77–80, 108ff.). For Hoffmann, Mozart's masses were, by and large, his weakest works; Haydn's, though full of musical ingenuity, contained melodies that destroyed the dignity of the sacred office and gave to the voices lines that were really intended for instruments. The great monuments of eighteenth-century sacred music, for Hoffmann, numbered but two: Handel's *Messiah* and Mozart's Requiem. Contemporary composers, when they deigned to write for the Church, wrote in a style that was far too theatrical, whereas those who composed sacred music in a truly serious manner (such as Michael Haydn) were undeservedly neglected.

Curiously, Hoffmann, whose essay included a history *en précis* of Church music from Bishop Ambrose to the contemporary scene (with Guido d'Arezzo, Franco of Cologne, Palestrina, Leonardo Leo and many others along the way), made no mention whatever of the Mass in C, which he had praised lavishly only a year before. Had he changed his mind about it, or did he not feel that it was yet appropriate to include Beethoven in the history of sacred music on the strength of one good piece?

Amid all the speculations about how the *Missa solemnis* is attached to the firmament of music history, one essay (written in 1959) took a uniquely subversive position. Theodor Adorno maintained that the Mass, by dint of being a large and substantial product of the composer's last years, had been uncritically accepted into the canon of masterpieces and therefore could no longer be examined objectively. Being the subject of adulation, rather than hard analysis, it had become 'alienated', detached from the cultural medium from which it had grown. Adorno agreed with Riezler that the music had not yet been subjected to careful scrutiny (1964: 160), but he was at least able to suggest a reason for this. The Mass, he claimed, was far from a typical Beethoven work – it was in some sense difficult to perceive it as a work by Beethoven at all – and thus it resisted analysis in the conventional terms of sonata style, motivic development or organic growth. Indeed, Beethoven himself may have had some inkling of the possible difficulties of later generations in understanding the work, when he placed the now famous subtitle 'Von Herzen – möge es wieder – zu Herzen gehn!' at the head of the score: an appeal to the heart, rather than to the brain, to accept a work which – as Adorno was at pains to repeat over and over – remains enigmatic and incomprehensible (1964: 148). In rejecting the appearance of unity of form and content it is typical of the 'late Beethoven demand for truth': but by being denied the conventional standards by which to judge the work, the listener becomes disorientated and incapable of objective evaluation. The *Missa solemnis* also shares with the other late works of Beethoven, as well as those of 'all great composers from Bach to Schoenberg', a tendency to fall back on archaic compositional techniques, further blocking access to the music.

Analytical studies

If Adorno was correct in identifying the rejection of Beethovenian harmonic–thematic logic as an essential compositional concern of the *Missa solemnis*, it is not surprising that sustained analytical investigation into the work is in short supply, or that conventional critical discussions contain frequent errors of analytical assessment. For instance, it was probably the hybrid form of the Kyrie (discussed later on) that led Mellers to judge a transitional passage in the second Kyrie to be 'more like a sonata development than a recapitulation' (1985: 303), despite the fact that it is quite normal for a recapitulation to contain harmonically transitional material (for example, what is frequently called a 'secondary development section'). In the final movement, the rhetorical force of the two outbursts of martial music was sufficient for Kirkendale to base his understanding of

Critical perspectives

the form upon them; on this basis he deemed the entire 'Dona' a 'rondo-
type movement (ABACA)' (1970: 696), disregarding the disposition of
themes in the three 'A' sections.

Nor are decisions made about harmonic analysis free from ambiguity.
While most writers have regarded the 'Et incarnatus' as being in the
D-Dorian mode, some writers have ascribed it to the F-Lydian (Cooper
1970: 245; Fiske 1979: 58). And Adorno, who warned us in the first place
of the elusiveness of the Mass, seriously underestimated the difficulty of
the Gloria's *Larghetto* ('Qui tollis') and the opening paragraphs of the
Credo when he asserted that harmonic progressions were hardly ever
problematic (1964: 148–9).

Though some critics have dealt with the musical behaviour of the Mass
at length, and others have turned to analysis in support of a historical
argument, only Donald Tovey's concert programme-note approaches the
work from the point of view of its musical form, a form which 'is as perfect
as the form of any symphony, or, in other words, of any purely abstract
music' (1937: 165). For Tovey, the analysis of sacred music was a simple
enough operation:

The way to grasp the form of this Mass is ... to ... take each clause of the text and
find out to what themes that clause is set. Where we find these themes recur, we
shall find cither that the composer has returned to the words associated with them,
or that he has some more than merely conventional reason for reminding us of those
words. It is through analysis on these lines that we are enabled to come to certain
general conclusions as to how Beethoven treats his text.   (1937: 165–6)

Of course, as Tovey's ubiquitous 'naïve listener' already knew, we need not
look for grand schemes unifying the motivic substance of the music. If the
text of, say, the Gloria or Credo is episodic, there is no reason why the
music should not also be so. And where the text is concise, for example, in
the Kyrie, the Benedictus and the 'Dona', one would naturally expect
abstract principles (such as we find in the forms of instrumental music) to
take over. Thus Tovey could call the second Kyrie a 'recapitulation'
(though he was careful not to describe the whole movement as being in
sonata form). And, following the most eloquent of his pronouncements
about freedom in musical form, he judged that the Benedictus and 'Dona'
were 'forms easily identifiable with certain types of sonata and concerto
form' (1937: 167, 178).

An essay by Tovey would, by definition, have little time for thematic
interrelationships. Most other discussions of Beethoven, however, cannot

7

dispense with them. Surprisingly, only one writer, Riezler, has had much to say about the thematic interrelationships in the Mass, and they make up only a minor part of his discussion of the work, itself confined to some dozen pages. For Riezler, a 'germinal motive of the greatest fertility', a rising leap of a fourth followed by a stepwise descent to the starting-point (see Ex.1.1), appears in bars 4–7 of the orchestral introduction to the Kyrie (1938: 190). Its development there and recurrence in other movements help unify the music.

Ex.1.1 Riezler's 'germinal motive' (Riezler 1938: 190)

Despite the attention given recently to Schoenbergian and Rétian thematic analysis, Riezler's idea of motivic unity has not been developed in any subsequent writings on the Mass. Joel Lester, in a study of the Kyrie autograph score, identified an 'Urmotif' which happens to be the same as Riezler's 'germinal motive'; but he did not investigate it beyond this movement (1970: 428–9).

Source studies

As with virtually all studies of Beethoven's creative procedures, the story of the *Missa solemnis* begins with Gustav Nottebohm, who pioneered sketchbook investigation in the second half of the nineteenth century. Nottebohm accurately identified three sketchbooks from the years 1819–22 and a pile of loose leaves that were used for the composition of the Mass, and his essays on these manuscripts contain the usual transcriptions selected from among the more striking (and legible) entries. But he was unable to reach any general conclusions about the genesis of the work, as he explained:

The sketches for the second Mass do not survive completely, and those that survive are found partly in a few sketchbooks, partly in a rather large number of leaves that do not belong together. It would add little to the history of the piece to follow the work on it step by step, to the extent that it survives and to the extent that this is possible. (1887: 148)

Though Nottebohm's pessimistic pronouncement did not actually deter research on the sketches for the Mass, it did discourage scholars from coming up with a comprehensive picture of how Beethoven put the Mass together. This picture was not appreciably improved in the 1950s and 60s when the Beethovenhaus embarked on a collected edition of the sketchbooks by publishing three of the smaller pocket-sized manuscripts in facsimile and transcription (Schmidt-Görg 1952–70). For not only were these so-called 'diplomatic transcriptions' produced with little consideration for musical sense (and hence virtually impossible to relate to any possible intentions on Beethoven's part), the manuscripts themselves – all part of the Beethovenhaus collection – gave little clue to the overall shaping of the piece. They were concerned almost entirely with parts of the Credo and the Benedictus, and opened the door to Beethoven's workshop for only part of the year 1820. Moreover, in each of these manuscripts there were places from which leaves had evidently been torn out, and some of the gaps were quite extensive, making it difficult to trace the continuity in Beethoven's compositional process.

The subsequent publication of one of the larger manuscripts, known as the 'Wittgenstein' Sketchbook, might have represented a major achievement in the field (Schmidt-Görg 1970–2). It was the first large-format sketchbook used for the Mass, and had been unknown to Nottebohm. But the transcription was again faulty; and the editor had not taken sufficient account of the leaves torn from the book (Winter 1975). Nor was the general shape of Beethoven's work on the Mass appreciably clarified by Otto Zickenheiner's substantial analysis of the Credo fugue and its sketches (Zickenheiner 1984).

With two publications in the mid-1980s, a much clearer picture of the sources for the Mass suddenly emerged. Robert Winter was the first to provide a chronology of work on the Mass, based on a detailed study of sketchbooks, loose manuscript leaves, and relevant conversation-book entries (Winter 1984).[3] A year later, a comprehensive guide to all the sketchbooks, prepared by three eminent Beethoven scholars, listed four large 'desk sketchbooks' and some dozen pocket sketchbooks, carefully dated and analysed for possible missing leaves (Johnson, Tyson and Winter 1985; Winter was responsible for describing the sketchbooks relating to the Mass). For Nottebohm's 'rather large number of leaves that do not belong together' a checklist was drawn up, with suggestions about possible relations between them.[4]

Very little research has been carried out on the autograph manuscript or the copies of the Mass prepared under Beethoven's supervision and subsequently corrected by him.[5] No scholarly edition of the finished work has yet appeared, though the primary sources for such a task have been accessible for a long time. The best available, published by Eulenburg *c.* 1964, ignores the three most important hand-written copies: Beethoven's *Handexemplar* (in which he worked out the last compositional problems), the dedication copy for Archduke Rudolph, and the *Stichvorlage* or copy from which the first edition was prepared. As Winter ruefully remarked, Beethoven's folksong settings 'have received as much attention from the scholarly community as has the *Missa solemnis*' (1984: 218).

A thorough account of the sources lies beyond the scope of this handbook. I shall give a brief survey of the sketchbooks in chapter 2, and discuss a few textual problems at the end of chapter 4. A glimpse of the early stages of the genesis of the Sanctus is offered in chapter 7.

2

Composition, performance and publication history

Background

Beethoven began to compose the Mass in D in the spring of 1819, on learning that Rudolph, Archduke of Austria, was to be made Archbishop of Olmütz in Moravia (now Olomouc, Czechoslovakia).

Rudolph (1788–1831), the youngest brother of Emperor Franz II, had been one of the three signatories to the contract of 1809 which guaranteed Beethoven a substantial annuity in return for remaining in Vienna. It was around this time that Rudolph became a pupil of Beethoven, receiving regular lessons in piano and composition for the next fifteen years.[1] He proved to be the most generous and reliable of the composer's patrons during his last two decades; in return, Beethoven dedicated a large number of major works to him, including the fourth and fifth piano concertos, three large piano sonatas, the Mass and the *Große Fuge* for string quartet. Of these, the Sonata in Eb ('Das Lebewohl', or 'Les adieux') represents the most personal expression of Beethoven's affection, its three movements being built around the programme of Farewell, Absence and Return which depicts the composer's feelings towards his pupil during the latter's enforced removal from war-torn Vienna in 1809–10.

News of Rudolph's elevation to the Archbishopric first circulated in the spring of 1819, and was evidently the direct stimulus for work on the Mass; nowhere can one find a more clear-cut relationship between an external event concerning Beethoven's life and his composition of a major work. A conversation-book entry of early April 1819 refers to the opening of the Kyrie: this now seems the most reasonable date to take for the start of its composition.[2] And Beethoven was making good progress on the music when, two months later, he proudly announced to his pupil and patron:

The day on which a High Mass composed by me will be performed during the ceremonies solemnized for Your Imperial Highness will be the most glorious day of

11

Table 1. *Principal manuscript sources for the Missa solemnis*

BH – Bonn, Beethovenhaus
BN – Paris, Bibliothèque Nationale

DSB – Berlin, Deutsche Staatsbibliothek
SPK – Berlin, Staatsbibliothek Preußischer Kulturbesitz
GdM – Vienna, Gesellschaft der Musikfreunde

Bodmer – Geneva–Cologne, Bibliotheca Bodmeriana
Schott – Mainz, Schott Publishers Archives

	Library, signature	Approximate date	Number of leaves surviving	Number of leaves original	Contents relating to the *Missa solemnis*
					Sources for the text of the Mass
T	DSB Aut. 32,52	spring 1819?	6	8	text of the Mass Ordinary, in Latin and parallel German translation, with marginal annotations on the meaning of individual words and phrases; a few sketches for the closing fugue of the Credo, and for the opening of the Sanctus. The texts of the Kyrie and Gloria are missing
		Standard format ('desk') sketchbooks (more detailed information in Johnson, Tyson and Winter 1985)			
S1	BH BSk1 (SBH 664)	spring 1819 – spring 1820	c.108	c.120	a few sketches for the Kyrie; a large number of sketches for the Gloria and Credo; rudimentary ideas for the Sanctus and Agnus Dei; facsimile and transcription, Schmidt-Görg 1970–2
S2	SPK Artaria 195	summer 1820– winter 1821	c. 106	120	sketches for the Credo, in particular the closing fugue, and for the Benedictus
S3	SPK Artaria 197	spring 1982 – autumn 1822	88	88	sketches for the Agnus Dei; a few entries for the Credo, and for the Benedictus
S4	SPK Artaria 201	winter 1821–2 – end of 1822	128	128	sketches for the 'Dona'; a few late sketches for the Credo
		Stitched pocket sketchbooks (see also Johnson, Tyson and Winter 1985)			
P1	DSB Artaria 180, pp.21–32, 111–12 BH 111 (SBH 669) Bodmer (1 double-leaf)	summer 1819	36	?	sketches for the Gloria (especially the closing fugue) and for the Credo
P2	BH 107 BH BSk 27	autumn 1819 – winter 1820	46	?48	sketches mainly for the Credo; a few entries for other movements; facsimile and transcription, Schmidt-Görg 1952–70, part 1
P3	BH 108	spring 1820	64	?68	sketches mainly for the Credo; a few entries for the Agnus Dei; facsimile and transcription, Schmidt-Görg 1952–70, part 2

P4	BH 109	autumn 1820 – winter 1821	38	?40	sketches mainly for the Benedictus; a few entries for the Sanctus and Agnus Dei; facsimile and transcription, Schmidt-Görg 1952–70, part 3
P5	DSB Grasnick 5	spring 1821	76	80	sketches for the Agnus Dei

Unstitched pocket gathering

G1	BH 110 (SBH 668)	spring 1819	4	?	a few sketches for the first three movements; several verbal inscriptions regarding the Credo
G2	DSB Artaria 180, pp.105–10	summer 1819	12	?16	sketches for the Credo (mainly the beginning); an entry for the closing fugue of the Gloria
G3	DSB Artaria 180, pp.37–42	?1820	12	?16	sketches for the closing fugue of the Credo
G4	DSB Artaria 180, pp.49–54	?1820	12	?16	sketches for the closing fugue of the Credo
G5	DSB Artaria 180, pp.47–8	?1820	4	?16	sketches for the closing fugue of the Credo
G6	DSB Artaria 180, pp.59–66, 89–90, 95–6	1820	24	32	sketches for the Credo
G7	DSB Artaria 180, pp.55–8, 91–4, 97–104	?summer 1820	32	32	sketches for the Credo and for the Sanctus
G8	DSB Artaria 180, pp.11–18, 67–72, 75–84	summer 1821	48	48	sketches for the Agnus Dei (mainly the 'Dona')
G9	DSB Artaria 205 part 6c	late summer 1821	16	16	sketches for the Credo; one entry for the 'Dona'
G10	BN MSS 51 part 3, 80, 99	autumn 1821	24	24	sketches for the Credo
G11	DSB Artaria 180, pp.3–10, 33–4 BN MS 51 part 7	late winter 1822	24	24	sketches for the Sanctus, Benedictus and 'Dona'
G12	DSB Artaria 205 part 6a	?autumn 1822	26	32	late revisions of details in the Kyrie, the Benedictus and (chiefly the) 'Dona'; entries for a 'Gloria in excelsis' in E major and an 'Offertor[ium]' 'Domine [Deus]'

Principal manuscripts of full scores

A	SPK aut. 1	?	autograph score of the Kyrie; facsimile edition = Virneisel 1965
	SPK Artaria 202	?1821–2	autograph score of the Credo, Sanctus and Agnus Dei
C1	GdM A 21	?1822–3	copy of entire score, with Beethoven's late compositional corrections
C2	GdM I 8281	early 1823	dedication copy of score, presented to Archduke Rudolph on 19 March 1990
C3	Schott	?1823–4	copy sent to B. Schotts Söhne, Mainz, in December 1824, for the preparation of the first edition

my life; and God will enlighten me so that my poor talents may contribute to the glorification of that solemn day. (Anderson 1961: 814–15)

In embarking on a work of such large proportions, Beethoven was obliged to shelve some of the compositional projects which had recently occupied him: a ninth symphony, ideas for which surface from time to time among the sketches of the period 1815–18, and a set of variations on a theme of Anton Diabelli, of which more than twenty variations and a concluding fugue had been quickly drafted in the early spring of 1819. Neither work was resumed until late 1822, by which time the sketching of the Mass was complete and only the preparation of a clean copy of the score remained.

But the composition of the Mass was itself interrupted at several points after the deadline for its completion – 9 March 1820, the date of Rudolph's installation as archbishop – had passed. One cannot be sure whether Beethoven had simply been unrealistic about completing the work within a year, or whether it had grown to a previously unimaginable size (it ended up more than twice the length of his earlier Mass in C), or whether personal circumstances (such as the ongoing litigation over custody of his nephew Karl) inhibited his concentration.

Once the deadline had passed, there was no longer any pressure to complete the work and Beethoven could divert his attention to other projects. The largest of these was a set of three piano sonatas for the Berlin publisher Adolf Martin Schlesinger and his son Moritz (Maurice), who had a music shop in Paris. The first (op.109, in E) was begun in the spring of 1820; the last (op.111, in C minor) was completed two years later. Work on the sonatas, the Overture 'zur Weihe des Hauses' (op.124) and some shorter compositions intermittently held up progress on the Mass between early 1820 and the end of 1822, for a total of approximately one year. Beethoven continued to make refinements to the work even as the first presentation copy of the score was being prepared, in the spring of 1823.

The composition of the Mass

The main musical sources of Beethoven's second setting of the Mass are given in Table 1. Before beginning work on it, he made a copy of the entire text in Latin with indications of the accentuation of every word, and with a line-for-line German translation (T). This document, which survives in the Deutsche Staatsbibliothek in Berlin, is of interest because it reveals three early stages of work not accounted for in the sketchbooks.

Firstly, it contains the minor emendations to the text of the Credo that correspond to the final version. In the phrases beginning 'Et in unum Dominum Jesum Christum' and 'Et in spiritum sanctum Dominum et vivificantem', the preposition 'Et' is replaced by the verb 'Credo': this, as we shall see, provided Beethoven with a new way of structuring the movement around its text.

Secondly, it contains numerous annotations on the meaning of the words, no doubt copied from the Latin–German dictionary in Beethoven's personal library. These annotations show that the composer took special pains to understand the text, rather than merely to follow the conventions of word-painting handed down from earlier Austrian settings of the Mass. Many are concerned, for example, with subtle differences between words with approximately the same meaning, namely 'terra' and 'mundus' (the world); or 'natum', 'genitum' and 'incarnatus' (born, begotten). Finally, it contains several rudimentary musical sketches, some of which may represent the earliest compositional work. (These include a remarkable draft of the opening of the Sanctus, which will be discussed later.)

The sketchbooks

By far the largest number of sources and amount of documentation of the Mass are devoted to the sketching and drafting of the work in one- or two-stave musical entries, or (more rarely) in short score. Because of its unusually long gestation, work on the Mass is found in four sketchbooks (S1 to S4), used consecutively from spring 1819 to autumn 1822, in which the composer would make notes at the desk beside his piano. These manuscripts were assembled at home from double-leaves (bifolia) of music paper, each leaf approximately thirty centimetres wide and twenty-four centimetres high and usually ruled with sixteen staves. These were folded to form a single bundle of some hundred or so pages, and crudely stitched together along the central fold for security. (One of the four manuscripts is made up of manuscript paper left over from other projects dating back as far as 1813; for more information on sketchbook construction, see Johnson, Tyson and Winter 1985.)

Parallel to these manuscripts is a series of half-size sketchbooks; these were put together in the same way, but using the *single* cut leaf of music paper as the unit of construction. These 'pocket sketchbooks', which fitted conveniently into the composer's large coat pockets, could be carried on walks and short journeys and were often used to work out specific problems (for example, the order of voice entries in the closing fugue of the Credo), as well as to record inspirations of a more general nature.

Though they all measure about fifteen by twenty-four centimetres, the pocket sketchbooks vary greatly in page number, containing anything from sixteen to eighty pages. Beethoven stitched the leaves of the larger groups together, but did not bother to do so with the smaller ones. Altogether five sewn pocket sketchbooks (P1 to P5) and fourteen unstitched gatherings survive from the period 1819–22; all but two of these latter group are devoted wholly, or largely, to the Mass (G1 to G12).

Besides these two categories of manuscript, there are sketches for the Mass on loose sheets of paper in various sizes and formats, as well as musical jottings in the conversation books. The latter are useful because they are among the few sketches which can be dated with any degree of accuracy; since they were sometimes copied into the sketchbooks, they can help determine the chronology of the sketches (see Winter 1984: 235–6).

Autograph scores and copies

Four of the five movements of the Mass survive in autograph full score (A). The autograph of the Kyrie, which consists of fifty pages in portrait format ruled with twenty staves per page, became separated from the rest of the autograph soon after Beethoven's death. The autograph of the Gloria disappeared around the same time, and has not since been traced. The last three movements together make up a 286-page manuscript in landscape format; this also has twenty staves per page, though the stave-ruling is narrower and the staves are more closely spaced.

Because of the large forces required, the autograph scores do not indicate the full orchestration of the Mass. The Kyrie is laid out in five groups of four staves: 1–4 woodwind; 5–8 brass and timpani; 9–12 strings; 13–16 chorus; and 17–20 solo voices. The Credo and Agnus are similarly planned, but with the chorus and solo voices switched around. The Sanctus, which contains a variety of unusual scorings, is laid out differently. Where blank space permitted, Beethoven indicated parts for other instruments (for example, the trombones at 'judicare' in the Credo); otherwise, the autograph score does not transmit the contrabassoon, trombone, double bass and organ parts.

Moreover, it represents no more than a working score. For an authoritative text of the work one must turn to the professionally-made copies, prepared under Beethoven's supervision and bearing further revisions in his hand. Three of these are paramount: a copy used by Beethoven to record the final details of the composition (C1; see Dorfmüller 1978: 347); the dedication copy presented to Rudolph on 19 March 1823 (C2); and a copy sent in January 1825 to the publishers Schott of Mainz (C3).

The marketing of the Mass: publication, performance

The genesis of the Mass bears witness to the longest, most arduous struggle in Beethoven's career as an artist. The steps he took to sell the work are likewise exceedingly complex, and they do not reveal the composer in the best light as a human being. The story of how the Mass was disseminated first in hand-written copies, and later in a printed edition, shows the composer double-dealing with publishers and often betraying the trust of his friends. It is amply documented in Thayer's biography (Thayer 1967: 784–95, 821–33, 853–6, 914–19) and soberly recounted by Solomon (1977: 271–4). A brief summary will be offered here.

Characteristically, Beethoven began making plans for the sale of the Mass well before it was completed. In March 1820, the Bonn publisher Nikolaus Simrock reached an agreement with him for the publishing rights, and paid a generous advance. Two years later, with the work fully sketched, Beethoven secretly persuaded another firm, C. F. Peters of Leipzig, to accept the work for a higher fee. As the completion of the Mass neared, Beethoven entered into negotiations with several more firms, including Artaria and Diabelli in Vienna, Schlesinger in Berlin, H. A. Probst in Leipzig and B. Schott's Sons in Mainz. Only in 1825 did he finally agree to give the work to Schott.[3]

In the midst of all these negotiations, and the completion of the work, Beethoven conceived the idea of sending invitations to heads of state in Europe, directors of choral societies, and other important personages (including Goethe and Cherubini) to subscribe to their own handwritten copy of the Mass. Ten letters of acceptance were received, and the Mass was copied out as many times in 1823.

One of these subscribers was Prince Nikolai Galitzin, who had already negotiated successfully with Beethoven for the purchase of three new string quartets (these were to be opp.127, 132 and 130). He also organized a performance of the work by the Philharmonic Society of St Petersburg. This was planned for a benefit concert for the widows of musicians, which normally took place around Christmas. But Galitzin did not receive his score from Beethoven until November; and the complexity of the work, especially the difficulty of the vocal parts, caused it to be postponed several times. It was finally given on 7 April 1824 (26 March in the Russian calendar), apparently to great acclaim (Fischmann 1970: 278–9).

In Vienna, the Mass was never performed complete in Beethoven's lifetime. Three movements (the Kyrie, Credo and Agnus Dei) were heard at the Kärntnertor Theatre on 7 May 1824, but the main attraction of this concert was the première of the Ninth Symphony; the programme was repeated a fortnight later, but with only the Kyrie of the Mass. These were Beethoven's last public concerts.

The first edition of the Mass, in full score and parts, appeared in the early spring of 1827, probably within days of Beethoven's death on 27 March; a piano–vocal score was issued at the same time. Beethoven had suggested to Schott that, to speed up the publication process, Gottfried Weber (editor of Schott's house magazine, *Cäcilia*), should be put in charge of correcting the proofs; but Weber had no intention of acting as Beethoven's *correcteur* (Schott 1985: 32–4). Unlike most of Beethoven's late works, the Mass was not carefully proofread by the composer and contains a large number of errors.

Despite the relatively large number of surviving sources, the Mass contains a number of textual problems that have not been satisfactorily resolved; some of these will be discussed in the following chapter.

3

Preliminaries to the analysis

For the *Missa solemnis*, as for virtually all music conceived for voices, the text must be the starting-point for a discussion of form. Indeed, it offers the simplest explanation for many of the basic features of Beethoven's Mass: the ternary shape of the Kyrie; the relatively diffuse design of the Gloria and Credo in comparison with the other movements; the fact that the Sanctus and Agnus Dei both end in different keys from those in which they began.

A detailed look at the text usually uncovers elements of what is often called 'word-painting', the musical characterization of a word or what it stands for. Some of these are self-evident, for example, rising and falling vocal lines for 'ascendit' and 'descendit', or the contrast between animated music in a high register and quiet sounds in a low register to express the opposition of 'Gloria in excelsis Deo' and 'et in terra pax'.

Beethoven often relied on established conventions whereby the music is sensibly related to the words without being dictated by them. The fact that the Gloria and Credo texts end with the same word, 'amen', may suggest that the endings were conceived along similar lines, but cannot actually determine the nature of the similarity; it is the observance of a long-standing tradition that makes both of these endings extended essays in polyphonic composition, that is, fugues.

Deeper investigation may uncover more subtle relationships between words and music; but at some point it must also be recognized that certain properties of the work can be appreciated for their musical qualities alone, however much their presence may depend upon the text. Sonata form is one such property; it plays a vital role in the Benedictus and 'Dona nobis pacem', as well as making the two 'Kyrie' sections of the first movement sufficiently different from one another to prevent us from labeling the movement 'A–B–A'. Motivic development, and the prolongation of structural tones (in the Schenkerian sense), are also important for an understanding of how the *Missa solemnis* is put together and how it makes its effect upon the listener. Of course, it would be a mistake to suppose that these musical features manifest themselves in the same way here as in, say, a sonata or symphony: rarely is the music allowed to run its course, independent of the text, even in passages where the text seems too brief to play a decisive shaping role. Nevertheless, it would be impossible to do justice to Beethoven's art, as exemplified by the *Missa solemnis*, without recourse to analytical concepts and the terminology which they require for clarity and precision.

No new 'theory' is being proposed here: various analytical viewpoints, taken together with the composition history of the Mass, its musical antecedents, and the liturgical symbols it reinterprets (Kirkendale's 'rhetorical tradition'), should provide a sufficiently broad perspective from which to appreciate it.

Not all these parameters bear upon the *Missa solemnis* at all times and in equal measure. It would be reasonable to suppose that the movements that set the longest text – the Gloria and Credo – demand a deeper investigation of the relationship of words (and liturgy) to music; whereas those built around a few words which must be repeated continuously to provide a basis for sustained musical argument – the Kyrie, Benedictus and Agnus Dei – are explicable more in musical terms. Though this preliminary standpoint may need modification, the requirements of an intelligent reading of the work are as varied as the techniques used by the composer to create it.

Beethoven and the Austrian mass tradition

How familiar was Beethoven with earlier sacred music? In 1808 he wrote to Breitkopf and Härtel, 'I think that I have treated the text [of the Mass in C, op.86] in a manner in which it has rarely been treated' (Anderson 1961: 189–90). This remark, which forms part of a postscript to a letter offering the Mass (and some other works) for publication, is probably best viewed as sales-talk for a musical work for which it would have been difficult to find a buyer. But it also suggests that Beethoven knew a reasonable cross-section of the contemporary repertory of masses, and had studied the text-setting carefully in them.

Documentary evidence of Beethoven's knowledge of sacred music is, however, rare. He possessed the scores of two of Joseph Haydn's six late masses, and may have known more of them, as well as Hummel's *Missa solemnis* in C of 1806, since they – like Beethoven's own Mass in C of 1807

– were all part of the series of 'Esterházy masses', performed at Eisenstadt to celebrate Princess Maria's nameday.

He may have also heard some of the masses by Michael Haydn or Mozart, since sacred music originating in Salzburg was frequently performed in Vienna. On the other hand, it is unlikely that these works would have had much influence on his later development. Moreover, a composer like Beethoven who had little sympathy for Catholic institutions and rarely attended church was unlikely to have heard many masses in their liturgical setting.[1]

Beethoven had heard early performances of Haydn's *Creation* and *Seasons*, and it is believed that their success around the turn of the century was the chief stimulus for his oratorio *Christus am Ölberge* (*The Mount of Olives*). He knew several of Handel's oratorios, and sketchbooks from various periods of his life contain copies of fragments from *Messiah*. But the sacred work which he seems to have cherished above all was Mozart's *Requiem*; he staunchly defended it when rumours of its doubtful authenticity reached Vienna in the mid-1820s. Recently, a Beethoven sketch-leaf came to light on which the Kyrie of the *Requiem* is written out in short score, with extensive annotations of its themes and formal sections (Churgin 1987). It is the only such 'analysis' by Beethoven, and probably dates from the period of work on the 'Et vitam venturi' fugue of the *Missa solemnis*. Thus the evidence linking Beethoven to the sacred music of the eighteenth century suggests that he was, or would have been, sympathetic to the ideas about Church music put forward by E.T.A. Hoffmann in 1814.

Analytical method

Since a large proportion of this study is devoted to analytical matters – form, motivic design, tonal coherence – a few general words on these topics may be in order here.

Sonata form, even if it had not been defined in the theory books of his time, was as much a reality for Beethoven throughout his career as it is for us today (Drabkin 1991b), and proved to be a major structuring principle in the *Missa solemnis* (as it was in Haydn's late masses of two decades earlier). It would be wrong, however, to lay too much emphasis on its tonal properties. In the music of Beethoven's later years, form is a function more of space and design than of tonality; in particular, the dominant is no longer *ex officio* the agent of tonal opposition. The use of alternative secondary keys – particularly those a major or minor third on either side of the home key – surfaces about 1800 and is prevalent throughout Beethoven's late period.

A related phenomenon is the blurring of the boundary between the development section and the recapitulation in sonata form, that is, the avoidance of a dramatic return of the opening theme following a long dominant preparation. Illustrations of this tempering of the reprise may be seen in both the Benedictus and the 'Dona' of the *Missa solemnis*.

Another analytical issue is modality versus tonality. Beethoven expressed his general thoughts on this in an entry made in his Tagebuch (diary) in 1818:

In order to write true church music, go through all the Gregorian chants [Kirchenchoräle der Mönche], etc. Also look there for the stanzas in the most correct translation, and for the most perfect prosody of all Christian–Catholic psalms and hymns in general. (Solomon 1982: 284)

However much has been made of some 'historical' aspects of the Mass, it can hardly be said that the music was influenced by Gregorian chant. In a passage such as the 'Et incarnatus' in the Credo, Beethoven's modality is so strongly tempered by polyphonic considerations that it has led some writers to label it Dorian (D-mode), others Lydian (F-mode). However, a harmonic language which can be described as 'religious' in quality pervades the work sufficiently to warrant the search for special features of major-minor tonality which are also common to other modes. One of Beethoven's commonest harmonic procedures in the *Missa solemnis* is to emphasize the subdominant: each of the three middle movements ends with a plagal cadence. Moreover, the blatantly anti-tonal flattened VII – the subdominant of the subdominant – becomes a part of Beethoven's harmonic vocabulary when a state of religious elation requires musical expression: passages from the Gloria of the Mass in C and the Act II finale of *Fidelio* are typical examples from the middle period that prepare the way for some of the unusual harmonies of the *Missa solemnis*, for instance at the end of the Gloria.

Mediant relationships must be considered close allies of the purely modal forces since they, too, dispense with the 'essential dissonance' of the seventh above the chord that resolves; where dominant-tonic resolutions are present, they often gain a devotional quality by the application of a 4–3 suspension of the dominant (for example, Kyrie, bar 3; Sanctus, bar 11).

The use of third-related keys also increases the chances of musical continuity being perceived more as a result of shared tones between adjacent chords than as the release of tension through the resolution of chords. This makes the concept of 'prolongation' of structural tones, as we find practised in Schenkerian analysis, a useful tool in the analysis of late Beethoven. In the Kyrie of the Mass, for instance, F♯ binds the music of the two 'Kyrie' sections – where it has a prominent role in the upper voice as the third step (the $\hat{3}$) of D major – with the 'Christe', which begins with F♯ as the $\hat{5}$ of B minor and ends with the same note reinterpreted as $\hat{1}$ of F♯ minor.

Motivic relationships have so often been misused in the analysis of late Beethoven that one might be tempted to side with Adorno, who claims that the Mass defiantly rejects the classical formulation of thematic logic as practised in the works of the middle period. A closer examination of the score, however, reveals that claims to the Mass's special position in Beethoven's *œuvre* need to be tempered. Yet the dangers of looking for an easy way out of the difficulty of finding unity (or 'integrity', to use Tovey's preferred term) in such a vast, problematic work have been so eloquently expressed that the analyst's responsibilities to the reader – the discovery and communication of significant relationships in the score – are now all the greater.

Textual problems

No published score of the *Missa solemnis* meets the present editorial standards of the musicological profession. The most recent redaction, published by Eulenburg (Hess 1964), includes a number of significant details from the autograph and first edition but fails to take note of the most important handwritten copies which Beethoven was able to correct (Winter 1984: 221). Although a thorough revision of the text is highly desirable, the task of collating the information in the primary sources lies beyond the scope of this handbook.

Two problematic areas – which invariably surface when performance of the Mass is discussed – will be considered here. Both concern the use of the solo voices versus the chorus: the first seven bars of 'Et incarnatus' (Credo, bars 125–31); and the entire 'Pleni' and 'Osanna' sections of the Sanctus (bars 34–78).

The first phrase of 'Et incarnatus' is assigned to the choral tenors in the autograph, but appears in the solo tenor part in subsequent copies and in the first edition. The important *Gesamtausgabe* (collected edition) of Beethoven's works, published in the 1860s, follows the autograph score and assigns the part to the choral tenors. But the solo version is currently preferred because it has Beethoven's authority: it represents his final decision on the matter, even if he did not bother to go back to the autograph score and enter the correction. Using the solo tenor also makes sense in context: it marks the beginning of a new section of the movement, one which the Austrian mass tradition distinguished by the use of a solo voice or voices.

On the other hand, the instrumental parts accompanying the tenor at bar 126 (violas, cellos and basses) lack the rubric 'nur einige Violinen', 'zwei Violen/Violoncelli', found later in the score, in bars 132–5. In other words, the change from choral to soloistic scoring at bar 125 is not aligned with a similar change in the orchestral parts. Furthermore, the solo tenor would enter as soloist in the bottom of his range, d–c^1, then as part of a quartet in a significantly higher register, g–g^1. And it is the higher of these that matches the next tenor solo at bar 143, 'Et homo factus est', where the home key of the Mass, D major, makes a dramatic return. The very different sounds produced by a voice in low and high registers is appropriate to the words; the 'Et incarnatus' conveys the mysteries of the virgin birth; whereas 'Et homo factus est' joyfully celebrates the existence of Christ as a human being. Beethoven may well have been after a different vocal sound, commensurate with the radically different instrumentation in the two passages: it is questionable whether using the same singer at bars 126 and 143 can produce an entirely satisfactory effect.

The voice parts of the 'Pleni' and 'Osanna' are assigned to the solo quartet in the primary sources, as in the first edition (and in all subsequent editions). This has often been perceived as conflicting not only with the jubilant character of the music – loud dynamics, fugal textures, fast tempos – but also with the traditional format of the mass, which would have invariably assigned the sung parts to the full chorus. Most modern performances use a chorus at this point, which suggests that Beethoven had either miscalculated the scoring or that the sources were misinterpreted by early copyists and editors.

I believe that the solo scoring is very likely the result of an ambiguity in the autograph score. To show why, it is necessary to study the layout of the manuscript.

Throughout the autograph of the Mass, the voice parts occupy the lowest staves. In the Kyrie, the choral parts (staves 13–16) lie above those of the soloists (staves 17–20); these groups are reversed in the Credo and Agnus Dei.

The beginning of the Sanctus, however, is a special case, because it requires far fewer staves to indicate all the performers: Beethoven was able, for the first time in the score, to assign separate staves to the three trombone parts and the double basses; for the opening orchestral ritornello, he needed only twelve staves. When the voices enter in bar 12 (page 3 of the autograph score), Beethoven sensibly placed the voice parts on staves 13–16: it would not have made sense to leave a gap of four staves between the instrumental and vocal parts. Staves 17–20 are thus blank throughout the 'Sanctus', and they remain blank in the 'Pleni sunt coeli':

staves	Credo	Sanctus, p.1 (beginning)	p.3 ('Sanctus')	p.8 ('Pleni')
1	flutes	clarinets	→	flutes
2	oboes	bassoons	→	oboes
3	clarinets	horn 2	→	clarinets
4	bassoons	horn 3–4	→	bassoons
5	horns 1–2	alto trombone	→	horn 2
6	horns 3–4	tenor trombone	→	horns 3–4
7	trumpets	bass trombone	→	trumpets
8	timpani	trumpets	→	timpani
9	1st violins	timpani	→	1st violins
10	2nd violins	violas	→	2nd violins
11	violas	cellos	→	violas
12	cellos/basses	basses	→	cellos/basses
13–16	solo voices	(blank)	voices	voices
17–20	chorus	(blank)	(blank)	(blank)

All Beethoven had to do was to indicate whether the parts on staves 13–16 in the Sanctus – on p. 3 of the autograph score, and (if necessary) again on p. 8 – were intended for soloists or for the chorus: but he *never specified them*. And a copyist who had already written out the Credo would naturally have interpreted this arrangement as calling for solo voices. It was not until the Benedictus that Beethoven needed separate staves for soloists and chorus, as follows:

13	soprano	solo
14	alto	
15	tenor	
16	bass	
17		soprano
18		alto
19	chorus	tenor
20		bass

Beethoven did not make his intentions entirely clear, therefore, and it is possible that the ambiguity resulted in subsequent copying errors.[2]

The Mass in D as a 'missa solemnis'

The title *Missa solemnis* is neither unique to Beethoven's Mass in D nor, in a strict sense, liturgically appropriate. From a liturgical point of view, a *Missa solemnis* comprises a setting of *all* parts of the mass service except for the readings, not just the five sections that make up the Ordinary. That relatively few such settings exist (those by Michael Haydn are the only ones Beethoven may possibly have known) is usually attributed to their limited application: a setting of the Proper and Ordinary for a particular feast could be performed, in principle, only once a year. But there are other factors as well: since musical settings usually involve considerable text repetition, the length of a complete polyphonic setting of the mass might well exceed an acceptable amount of time for its celebration. Certain masses included settings of some extra music; Cherubini's C major *Messe solenne* of 1816, for instance, includes an Offertorium ('Laudate Dominum omnes gentes') and an 'O salutaris hostia' inserted between the Sanctus and the Agnus Dei.

In general, however, the mass setting was able to gain the status of a musical form precisely because it was restricted to a stable number of elements. The tradition of setting only the five items of the Ordinary had existed for a long time; where it was abandoned, for example, by Michael Haydn, the extra musical items are – musically – of secondary importance. Beethoven briefly entertained the idea of including an offertory in the *Missa solemnis*, but did not get beyond sketching the first few bars.

The notion that a *Missa solemnis*, from a composer's point of view, might instead signify a more elaborate composition – one which takes longer than average to perform, or which requires exceptional performing forces – was current in the latter half of the eighteenth century and in the first part of the nineteenth. Mozart called his K.337 (performed in 1780 in Salzburg) a *missa solemnis*; the same designation for K.139, written in 1768 (at the age of twelve) for a Viennese orphanage, originated from his father. Joseph Haydn did not use the term for any of his Esterházy masses, but Hummel did for his Mass in C major, which was performed at Esterház in 1806. Seen in this light, Beethoven's second setting of the mass, which requires a large orchestra even by the standards of his own symphonies and which lasts for well over an hour, fully deserves to be identified with the genre with which it has become almost synonymous.

When Beethoven advertised the completed Mass in D to prospective subscribers, he stressed that it could also be performed as an oratorio, that is, outside the context of a church service. Since the St Petersburg première of 1824, where it had already been billed and talked about as an oratorio, the vast majority of performances have taken place in the concert hall. As we shall see in the last chapter of this study, a number of features of the music are highlighted by its performance as a self-contained choral work, that is, as a succession of five movements, rather than with intervening sung (and spoken) elements.

4

Kyrie

Assai sostenuto. Mit Andacht   [with devotion], ¢, 85 bars
Kyrie eleison.   Lord, have mercy.

Andante assai ben marcato, $\frac{3}{2}$,   **43 bars**
Christe eleison.   Christ, have mercy.

Tempo I, 95 bars
Kyrie eleison.   Lord, have mercy.

In all settings of the Mass the simple, symmetrical text of the Kyrie results in some kind of three-part form. In 'cantata' masses the Kyrie may comprise three self-contained musical numbers; in Bach's Mass in B minor, the outer 'Kyrie' sections are materially different movements set in different keys, linked only by being choral fugues. But in late Classical masses, such as those of Joseph Haydn, the Kyrie is usually in sonata form, with the setting of 'Christe eleison' normally assigned to a theme in the second group ('Nelson' Mass), or to the development (*Mariazellermesse*), and thus contrasting with the outer 'Kyries' in tonality and mood. Beethoven's Mass in C follows this practice: the 'Christe' occupies the second group, though in the relatively distant key of E major.

In the *Missa solemnis*, the form of the Kyrie derives from both traditions. On the one hand, the 'Christe' is set in a different metre and tempo; Beethoven makes the distinction more noticeable by stark contrasts in texture and phrase construction. He also begins the second 'Kyrie' with the same grand gesture as the first, a feature which has probably given rise to the notion of the movement as a musical representation of church architecture with the opening twelve bars of its outer sections heard as analogous to the supporting pillars (Marx 1863: ii, 246).

On the other hand, the first 'Kyrie' is open-ended, like a sonata exposition, its tonal and motivic arguments completed by the second; and, as we shall see, these arguments have a bearing on the material on which the 'Christe' is built. The interest of the movement may be said to reside in the conflict between a liturgically conservative formal plan and the progressive symphonic forces it is intended to contain.

The tension between form and development is observable in the general tonal plan of the movement, given in Example 4.1. On the one hand, the 'Christe' is set in B minor, and thus the end of the first 'Kyrie' must lead in this direction, much like the bridge or transition between the two subject groups of an exposition. But the relative minor was rarely chosen as a secondary key for a sonata-type argument, and its presence (or imminence) at the end of the 'Kyrie' weakens that argument. On the other hand, the bridge does actually pass through the more conventional dominant, at bar 57; this dominant is counterbalanced in the second 'Kyrie' by a strong subdominant presence at bars 140–64, later echoed in bars 192–200. This equilibrium between dominant and subdominant helps us relate the two outer sections to one another, in much the way we relate exposition to recapitulation in sonata form.

The first 'Kyrie' (bars 1–85)

This part of the movement unfolds in two large paragraphs, the first of which is divided into two statements in the home key. The first statement, in effect an orchestral opening (bars 1–20), presents many of the movement's thematic ideas; it also touches on its most important harmonies, namely the relative minor (bar 3) and its dominant F♯ major (bar 17), before closing in the tonic. The second statement (bars 21–49) introduces the chorus and solo singers as contrasting forces, and begins to develop the themes.

Ex.4.1 Harmonic outline of the Kyrie

The second paragraph (bars 50–85) moves away from the tonic, aiming first at the dominant (bar 59) before going on to prepare the relative minor by stretching out its dominant with a series of 'neighbour harmonies' in B minor (bars 67ff.): V–i–V, V – V of V – V, V–iv–V.

The importance of third-relationships is underscored by the very first chord-change in the piece, from D major to B minor. It is largely this impulse which gives us the tonal contrast between the 'Kyrie' and the 'Christe', and more immediately provides us with thematic growth in the piece.

Despite the brevity of the text, the thematic material of the Kyrie gains its rhythm in exactly the same way as that of the longer movements, namely from the accentuation of the words: *Ky*-ri-*e* e-*le*-i-*son* (or e-*lei*-son). Moreover, the isolation of single words – 'Kyrie', 'Christe' and 'eleison' – generates additional thematic material, thus justifying an expansion of the form. This technique, which is used elsewhere in the Mass, enables Beethoven to provide thematic contrast within the section without actually having a well-defined second-subject group.

The initial thematic development on the word 'Kyrie' is illustrated in Example 4.2. A thrice-repeated D major chord (a) leads to the entry of the solo tenor, which adds a melodic dimension to the rhythm by leaping a third (b). The soprano expands this interval to a diminished fifth (c), which suggests a resolution to the tonic. The alto then provides the expected harmonic resolution, at the same time increasing the melodic character of the figure with a three-note descent (d).

It is this setting, ending with g^1-f♯^{1}, which furnishes the basis of the new 'eleison' figure (e) and thus brings us full circle to the beginning of the movement (f): for although the notes of Riezler's 'germinal motive' have been rotated, the 'voice-exchange' between melody and bass enables us to make the connection between it and the new figure. The perception of the four notes as a unit is further promoted by the tonic pedal point, which completes the sonority of the alternating subdominant and tonic chords.

These materials are developed further in the second paragraph (see Ex.4.3). Since the oboe solo beginning on the upbeat to bar 50 (b) begins the paragraph, we hear it as a new theme; yet in reality it is a development of the 'eleison' figure, and with each pair of notes preceded by a leap that can be traced back to the violin accompaniment figure in bars 12–14 (a). The first 'extra' note, d^2, is simply an interior tonic pedal-point which has now become part of the melody (c). The second interpolation, e^2, is non-harmonic, and can be viewed either as a neighbour to d^2 or as a

Ex.4.2 (a) bars 21–3   (b) bars 23–5   (c) bars 27–9
        (d) bars 31–3   (e) bars 33–5   (f) bars 2–6, outline

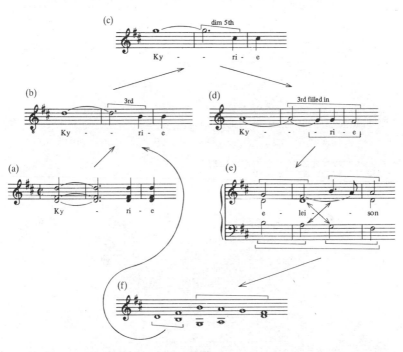

passing note between d^2 and $f\sharp^2$. Both options are worked out in turn: the first two statements of the oboe figure are answered by the choral 'Kyrie' and 'eleison' in unison on D, so that the e^2 in effect returns to its starting point (d). But when the clarinet takes over this figure, and the choral line moves up by step D–E–F$\sharp$, there is a change of harmony which makes the e^2 consonant: this focusses our attention equally on the chorus and the clarinet, with two melodic strands pointing towards the strategic F$\sharp$ major chord in bar 55 (e). Having reached the climax of the modulation, Beethoven ceases to develop the 'eleison' figure further, and simply lets the various accompanying instruments adapt its crotchet rhythm to the subsequent harmonies, reducing it to its original dimensions as a three-note motif (compare (a) and (f) in Ex. 4.3). The last residues of this motif provide the impulse for the countersubject to the 'Christe' motif (g).

Ex.4.3   (a) bars 12–14   (b) bars 49–51   (c) bar 49–50
          (d) bars 50–1   (e) bars 54–5   (f) 81–6
          (g) bars 86–8

'Christe' (bars 86–128)

The most obviously recognizable features of the 'Christe' are those which contrast it with the 'Kyrie': key and mode, tempo and metre, and vocal textures. In addition, its phrase-structure is based on a different principle: it develops not by presenting and expanding cadential patterns (I–IV–V–I), but by assembling motivically concise units, usually two bars long and expressing some form of dominant-to-tonic relation. In developing by the accumulation of short musical segments, the 'Christe' behaves not like a self-contained B-section of predictable dimensions (such as the 'trio' of a minuet), but instead puts an indefinite amount of space between the two Kyries: its overall length cannot be guessed from the nature of the thematic materials. In this respect it fulfils the most important role of a sonata-form development: to distance the second 'Kyrie' from the first. Hence the 'Christe' contributes to the formal ambiguity of the movement described earlier.

The unit of construction is a two-bar pattern in which the words 'Christe' and 'eleison' form the basis of opposing figures in counterpoint. The permutation of these voices in the solo parts, and later in the chorus, is the chief method of continuation. Repetition at the same harmonic level (bars 86–7, 88–9, 90–91 in B minor) provides stability; transposition to different levels (bars 92–3 and 94–5 in D, bars 96–7 and 98–9 in G) merely lifts the music to a new stasis.

True development takes place in bars 99ff., where the 'Christe' figure is temporarily abandoned and the harmony pushes towards a cadence in G major. But when the chorus enters, at bar 104, the harmonic phrasing reverts to the two-bar dominant-to-tonic pattern established earlier, thus weakening the arrival of G at bar 105 as a resolution. The re-entry of the soloists on the original harmonic level (V–I of B minor in bars 113–14) finally leads to a cycle of fifths which aims initially to close in B minor; but by the process of voice-exchange with chromatic alteration in bars 120–1, whereby B is replaced B♯, its final cadence is diverted to F♯ minor (see Ex.4.4a). The close of the 'Christe' can thus overlap with the reprise of the 'Kyrie', the majestic opening of the movement simply absorbing a cadential F♯ minor triad that has been reduced to its third F♯–A (Ex.4.4b).

The second 'Kyrie' (bars 129–223)

The identity of the two 'Kyrie' sections is preserved until the chorus enters at bar 140. Now the entire vocal exposition is repeated with modifications – in G major, the subdominant (bars 140–64). This is a typical procedure in sonata-form reprises, even in Beethoven's late music (Sonatas opp.110–11, first movements; Quartet op.131, finale), and the subsequent transition duly develops the oboe theme to bring the tonality back to D major (bars 165–89).

Ex.4.4 (a) bars 118–28, outline   (b) bars 126–30

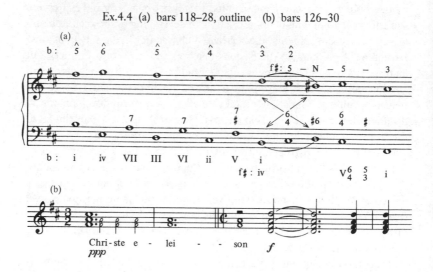

This creates the problem of how to round off the music in a satisfactory way. Ordinary sonata form achieves this, of course, by recapitulating the second subject group in the tonic, thereby 'resolving' what is sometimes called the 'large-scale dissonance' between the tonic and the contrasting key (Webster 1980: 498). But there has been no 'second subject' that might be so treated, and to introduce a new theme – or to restate material from the 'Christe' – would undermine the overall ternary design. Further material is needed, but not a restatement of an important theme that could be perceived as a substitute for a second subject.

Beethoven's solution is to develop an idea from the first 'Kyrie', but one which is thematically 'neutral', that is, having no value as a melody in itself. This takes the form of a turn-figure G♯–A–B–A (bar 193) and its inversion B–A–G♯–A (bar 201), which recalls the G♯–A in the bass supporting the secondary dominant and its resolution in bars 46–7. These turn-figures are developed in a pair of phrases leading to a cadence at bar 206. With the tonic grounded, an earlier theme is now recalled to round off the

Ex.4.5 (a) bars 212–23 (b) outline of above

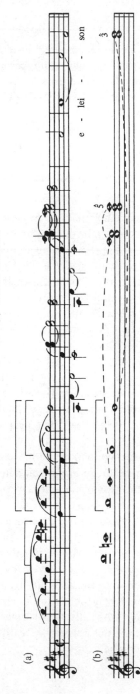

movement: the oboe melody (see Ex.4.3b). The development of this theme in bars 207ff., in effect the coda of the movement, allows the 'germinal motive' to revert to its original shape (see Ex.4.5). The pairs G–F♯ and B–A are first treated sequentially, rising to higher levels A–G + C♮–B (bars 211–12) and B–A + D–C♮ (bars 213–14). The last pair initiates a downward step progression that brings back B–A (oboe, bar 215) and G–F♯ (clarinet, bar 216). While G–F♯ is repeated to bring the melodic movement to rest, the chorus summarizes the four-note descent with a simple, quiet leap between the two notes of the tonic chord, A and F♯.

The Kyrie is in every respect a quiet movement. It reaches *fortissimo* in several places, but only to provide points of contrast for the predominating *piano* and *pianissimo* dynamics, not to drum home a particular theme, harmony or phrase of the text. In form, too, it seems static: as a hybrid of the sonata and A–B–A, it avoids dramatizing crucial points, namely the arrival of a second subject in a contrasting key and the beginning of the recapitulation (by a preparatory dominant retransition). Even the coda, traditionally a rousing part of the form, proceeds peacefully and ends with the melody suspended on the third step of the scale.

It captures a mood similar to that of the Kyrie of the Mass in C (which can ultimately be derived from Haydn's *Harmoniemesse*), but the realization is finer. Because of its more reserved harmonic structure (I–vi–I, rather than I–III–I as in the earlier Mass), it allows the 'Christe' to be felt more as an integral part of the movement, rather than being heard as a necessary contrast.

The orchestration confirms the conservative outlook of the movement without reverting to the eighteenth-century aesthetic of string-orchestra domination. The oboe is given the principal woodwind solos, with the clarinet used as an alternative timbre at the same level and the flute in a higher register; the horns, though melodically prominent, are restrained by the overtone series to a much greater extent than they are in earlier symphonic works (and in later movements of the Mass). Finally, the orchestral sonorities are related to the tonality of the movement (for illustration, see Ex.9.4). This property, which was crucial to the structure of the earlier Classical symphony, gives the Kyrie the sense of stability necessary before the full energy of Beethoven's inventiveness surfaces in the later movements of the Mass. By being given this reassurance early on, so to speak, the listener is better prepared for what is to come.

5

Gloria

Allegro vivace – meno allegro – Tempo I, $\frac{3}{4}$, 229 bars

Gloria in excelsis Deo,
  et in terra pax hominibus
  bonae voluntatis.

Laudamus te, benedicimus te,
  adoramus te, glorificamus te.

Gratias agimus tibi propter
  magnam gloriam tuam.

Domine Deus, rex coelestis
  Deus, pater omnipotens,
Domine fili unigenite, Jesu Christe
Domine Deus, agnus Dei, filius
Patris,

Glory to God in the highest,
  and on earth peace to men
  of good will.

We praise you, we bless you,
  we worship you, we glorify you.

We give thanks to you for
  your great glory

Lord God, king of Heaven,
  God the all-powerful father,
Lord, only-begotten son Jesus
Christ,
Lord God, lamb of God, son of the
father,

Larghetto,

qui tollis peccata mundi,
  miserere nobis;
qui tollis peccata mundi,
  suscipe deprecationem nostram;
qui sedes ad dexteram patris,
  (o) miserere nobis.

$\frac{2}{4}$, 80 bars

who takes away the sins of the world,
  have mercy on us;
who takes away the sins of the world,
  hear our pleading;
who sits at the right of the father,
  (o) have mercy on us.

**Allegro maestoso, $\frac{3}{4}$ – Allegro, ma non troppo e ben marcato, C –
poco più allegro, ¢ – Presto, $\frac{3}{4}$, 260 bars**

Quoniam tu solus sanctus Dominus;
  tu solus altissimus
  Jesu Christe, cum sancto spiritu
in gloria Dei patris, amen.

For you alone are holy, Lord;
  you alone are the highest,
  Jesus Christ, with the Holy Spirit
in the glory of God the father, amen.

The principles of development and recapitulation, so central to the design of Classical music, cannot easily be applied to settings of the Gloria and Credo in which the composer makes a special effort to come to terms with the meaning of the words. Compared to the simple, brief texts of the other sections of the mass, the Gloria and Credo are too long to be set

37

conveniently as single movements; the 'cantata mass' solution, whereby each is divided into several movements (nine plus nine, for instance, in Bach's Mass in B minor) is an obvious way out of the difficulty.

Length, however, is only a part of the problem; the ordering of ideas in the texts is not always conducive to the type of development which the language of late eighteenth- and early nineteenth-century music could accommodate naturally. The Gloria is the shorter of the texts, yet it is in some respects more difficult to set. All its statements are addressed to God; but the diversity of their construction, and of the sentiments they convey, makes it difficult for a composer to give due attention to the words while at the same time formulating a musically coherent statement.

For example, the very opening acclamation gives most musical settings their principal, joyous mood; but the continuation expresses a sentiment of threefold opposition:

Glory in the highest to God
Peace on earth to men of good will

A musical setting which takes account of this distinction would have to use contrasting textures, dynamics and, most probably, themes: thematic opposition would then be established at a very early stage in the work, with a vast territory yet to be covered.

A difficulty of another order can be seen in the following paragraph, made up of four parallel constructions. Syntactically, these might seem well suited to Classical musical procedures such as sequence, pairs of antecedent–consequent phrases, or mere repetition. But the statements themselves are far from equivalent in sentiment: the third ('adoramus te') suggests wonderment while the fourth ('glorificamus te') reverts to the 'glory' of the opening words. Thus literal repetition would be difficult to justify, and continuous musical development in one direction would also be at odds with the text; antecedent–consequent phrasing would not work for the second pair of phrases.

A problem on a still higher level concerns the organization of the movement into large sections. If the details of the text require musical contrast from one phrase to the next, then the idea of a 'movement' – in the sense of a single tempo for the entire text – must break down; yet there was a long tradition, related to 'cantata mass' procedure, of dividing the Gloria into sections. In the late eighteenth-century Austrian mass, the division of the text at either 'Gratias agimus tibi' or 'Qui tollis peccata mundi' (and again at 'Quoniam tu solus sanctus') created a three-part form ternary in at least one sense: the 'Quoniam' always returned to the opening key of Gloria, though rarely to the opening theme (the 'Nelson' Mass is exceptional).

Either demarcation of the 'middle' section is, however, problematic. Most settings treat the three statements preceding the 'Quoniam' as a unit, syntactically unified by the personal pronoun 'qui' which begins them, and referring back to the three preceding phrases beginning with 'Domine'. In other words, the standard division of the text at 'Qui tollis' divides the subject from the rest of the sentence. Making 'Gratias' and 'Quoniam' the two dividing points makes better grammatical sense; however, this runs the risk of the middle section outweighing the outer sections, something at odds with Classical decorum.

A compromise would be to have a four-part Gloria, with both 'Gratias' and 'Qui tollis' marked by changes in tempo (Haydn's *Heiligmesse* and *Theresienmesse*), or a middle section that is clearly subdivided by changes of texture or modality (*Mariazellermesse, Harmoniemesse*). The size of the middle section may then be offset by a lengthy fugue on 'Cum sancto spiritu' or 'In gloria Dei Patris':

A	B1 – B2		C1 – C2
Gloria	Gratias	Qui tollis	Quoniam (fugue)

But this would still leave a relatively slight opening section.

It seems that Beethoven was sensitive to these issues, for he created a form for the Gloria which both accommodates the conventions of Classical settings and takes account of the difficulties that arise from their observance. Consider, for instance, the recurrences of the prominent opening figure – the 'Gloria' motif – at various points and in different keys: at bars 66 (in D), 174 (in Eb), 210 (in F) and 525 (in D). On the face of it, these suggest the ritornello principle of Baroque concerted music; but a quick calculation of the intervals between these points and a survey of the intervening musical material are enough to show that such an interpretation is unsatisfactory. So how are they to be explained?

The easiest way is to relate them to the structure of the text, for they correspond to the beginnings of sentences: 'Laudamus te', 'Domine Deus' (twice) and the non-liturgical return of the opening 'Gloria in excelsis deo'. If we take these recurrences as grammatical signposts defining sections of the music, we can then understand the form of the Gloria as both accommodating the traditional design of the movement (with clear divisions at 'Gratias', 'Qui tollis' and 'Quoniam') and corresponding to the syntactic form of the text.

This duality of form raises a new question: are we meant to hear the Gloria in musical sections, or as a series of verbal statements? This is a problem here because Beethoven does not confine changes in tempo to the beginning of the 'Gratias' and 'Qui tollis', but returns to the tempo of the opening 'Gloria' in between. The extra tempo change has fundamental implications for the 'plot' of the movement. The 'Gratias', despite its slower tempo and change of scoring (solo voices, woodwind), cannot be thought of as a section of the movement in the usual sense: it is in the same metre as the 'Gloria', and it is open-ended, being cut short by 'Domine Deus' that returns to Tempo I. By comparison, the 'Qui tollis' emerges as a stronger area of contrast, in a noticeably slower tempo (in duple time) and bound by fast music (in triple time) on either side. On the other hand, it would be misleading to say that the music divides into three sections, with the 'Gratias' understood as part of the opening section: for the Tempo I, despite the thematic recurrences, is set predominantly in flat keys and does not recapture the jubilant mood of the opening.[1]

The difficulties encountered in marking the boundaries in the middle of the Gloria may help us understand its form as a whole. For instead of being divided, conventionally, into sections, it contains a number of points of change which create disruption on different levels. The strongest of these mark the beginnings of 'Qui tollis' and 'Quoniam', with 'Gratias' and the 'In gloria' fugue being somewhat less sharply defined. Other changes, not always involving tempo or tonality, encourage the listener to make lower-order divisions in the Gloria as the music proceeds, resulting in a less predictable, more fluid form, but one that is no less carefully organized.

Most of the 'extra' subdivisions are prompted by textual considerations: in the highlighting of a phrase, or sometimes just a single word, Beethoven either brings out that portion of text or makes the following phrase stand out. 'Et in terra pax' (bar 43) illustrates a simple subdivision, with modest change of texture, used to contrast the noisy celebration of God's glory 'in the highest' with peace 'on earth'.

A more complicated situation is created by the four phrases of the 'Laudamus te' group. Beethoven takes an original line here by recalling the opening 'Gloria' motif rather than introducing a new theme. In common with late Classical practice, he sets 'Adoramus te' mysteriously, but then recognizes that it would be too disruptive to depart from the basic mood of the group for just these words, rushing back to a noisy 'Glorificamus te'.

(This is precisely what happens in Beethoven's earlier Mass: the tonal contrast between C and B♭ is startling but, I believe, ultimately unsatisfactory.)

The problem is solved by making the 'Adoramus te' an ending, the final, quiet phrase of the 'Laudamus' group. The 'Glorificamus te' then initiates a new, fugal passage (bar 84) in which the jubilant mood of the opening 'Gloria' is appropriately recalled. The fugato spills over into a second setting of the 'Laudamus' group (bar 94), rounded off by another quiet 'Adoramus te' and followed by a second fugato on 'Glorificamus' (bar 104).[2]

Beethoven insists upon giving full weight to every word that holds a special meaning for him: 'adoramus', 'omnipotens' (bars 186–90) and 'miserere' (especially bars 292–305), to mention the three most obvious examples. To integrate such emphases successfully, he is obliged to write longer passages building up to or leading away from these 'highlights'; and in doing so the parts of the text which do not require special treatment must, nevertheless, be given a musical setting which creates good proportions for the whole. This is one justification for the closing fugue being fully a third of the total length of the piece, and ultimately explains a liturgically extraneous coda in which the opening acclamation and its music are recapitulated at breakneck speed.

In listening to the Gloria, then, one is conscious of 'sectionalism', but of a kind that exists on almost as many levels as there are sections. This makes it easier for Beethoven to 'divide and conquer' the text of the Gloria without detracting from the overall cohesiveness of the music: the very difference in the degree of separation between sections accounts, in great part, for its unity as a whole. Table 2 offers one possible way of showing the movement's subdivision. It is not intended as a formal outline, but rather as giving some idea of the different degrees of independence of certain parts of the text. Broadly speaking, the Gloria divides into three parts, of which the central 'Qui tollis' is the shortest and least susceptible to subdivision at an intermediate level.

Gloria in excelsis Deo

Since the subsections of the Gloria are interdependent, and none can be taken as a complete musical statement, Beethoven was obliged to devise a way of giving each more weight, thus allowing the music to develop and not merely become a string of ideas. Initially this was facilitated by text

Table 2. Hierarchical divisions in the Gloria

primary	secondary	tertiary	lower-level	Remarks (grounds for partitioning; against partitioning)
1 Gloria				beginning of movement;
			43 Et in terra	new theme, quieter; same tempo and key
			66 Laudamus te	return of Gloria motif; same tempo and key
			84 Glorificamus (i)	new idea, fugato; same tempo and key
			104 Glorificamus (ii)	new key (G), new fugato relation
	128 Gratias			new key (Bb→Eb), theme, dynamics, scoring, tempo; same metre
		174 Domine Deus		Tempo I°, main 'Gloria' theme; same key (Eb)
			196 Domine filius	new theme, quieter; same tempo, harmony already transitional
			210 Domine Deus	new key (F), return to main 'Gloria' theme; same tempo
230 Qui tollis				new theme, dynamics and scoring, major tempo change; same key
			253 Qui tollis	new key (D); same theme and tempo
			269 Qui sedes	new key (Bb); same tempo and pacing
310 Quoniam				new theme, dynamics and scoring, major change in tempo
			345 Cum sancto spiritu	new theme, rhythmic caesura; same tempo and key
	360 In gloria			new theme (closing fugue), change in tempo; same key, scoring
			428 Cum sancto/Amen	rhythmic caesura, change in texture; same theme, tempo and key
			459 Amen	new theme, change in scoring; minor change in tempo
		525 Gloria		return to opening theme, new tempo, new key and scoring

repetition; subsections comprise two statements of their text instead of one: 'Gloria in excelsis Deo' (bars 5, 29); 'Et in terra pax'. (43, 54); and the 'Laudamus' group. The latter parts of the text already contain repeated phrases (for example, 'Domine Deus', 'Qui tollis', 'miserere nobis') and thus can accommodate musical repetition more naturally.

For most listeners, the opening 'Gloria in excelsis Deo' offers the first suggestion in the *Missa solemnis* of festive Baroque music in general and Handelian oratorio in particular. The rising scale-figure $d^2-e^2-f\sharp^2-g^2-a^2$ recalls the mood of both the 'Amen' finale and the 'Hallelujah' Chorus of *Messiah* (Schmitz 1963: 320–1) largely because it takes place in precisely the register in which the trumpet becomes a melodic instrument, that is, above the eighth partial in the overtone series.[3]

The working-out of this figure (see Ex.5.1) is unusual, yet no less Beethovenian in its logic. It rises to the fifth of D major, then falls back through the notes of the tonic triad (a). The normal 'development' of a tonic chord would be a move to the dominant, and this is achieved by transposition, creating opposition between the fifths d^1-a^1 and a^1-e^2 (b). Closure back to the tonic now becomes easier: the e^2 can fall by step to d^2, motivating the quick, staccato 'Gloria' figure (c).

The resulting e^2-d^2 (supported by V–I harmony) is raised to a higher position by sequence, $g^2-f\sharp^2$. Beethoven first proceeds homophonically, with E–D shifted to the bass by voice-exchange (d). Then, as further development, we hear the same idea heterophonically, producing a class of E against D (e). The 'resolution' of this clash can take place only when E and D become part of the same chord, that is, a secondary dominant (f), which then leads to a sequential harmony before returning to its starting point. Bars 1–28 can thus be seen as a presentation and development; the repeat of the opening theme (bars 29ff.) and its subsequent rounding-off summarizes these procedures.

Ex.5.1   (a)   bars 1–5, outline   (b)   bars 5–16, outline   (c)   bar 17
          (d)   bars 17–18   (e)   bars 21–2   (f)   bar 23

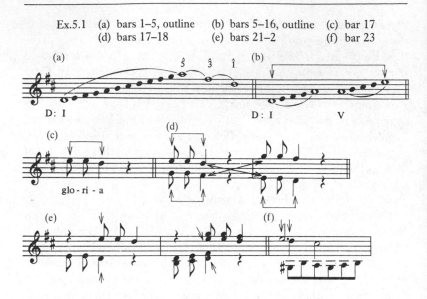

The 'Et in terra' helps to separate the 'Gloria' music from its repeat at 'Laudamus te'. Its quiet theme is stated first in D major, then a fourth higher (bar 59). This shift to the subdominant is not so much a modulation as a way of allowing the opening music to return, without it actually seeming like the outcome of what has come before: it is as if the movement begins again at bar 66.

The arrangement of the 'Laudamus' group takes the concept of dual presentation one stage further by emphasizing the last of the four text elements, 'Glorificamus te'. The reasons for this, as explained above, have to do with the setting of 'Adoramus te' which, for full effect, is treated as the last element in a group of three, rather than the third in a group of four. In treating the 'Glorificamus te' as a new beginning, marked by fugal entries, Beethoven follows the same procedure as for 'Et in terra pax' by initiating a second fugato in the subdominant. This time, however, the harmony is allowed to develop further and continues to drift towards the flat side.

The chord on C, whose pivotal position is clarified by the chromatic change from E♮ to E♭, becomes the signal for the new tonality, tempo and scoring for the 'Gratias'.

Ex.5.2 bars 117–30, outline

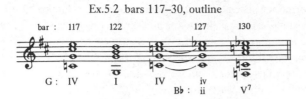

The 'Gratias' begins as if Beethoven were treating it as a separate section: only the $\frac{3}{4}$ metre is held over, and even the identity of the time signature is masked by a change to a much smoother articulation in two-bar groups, so that the music resembles a quasi-pastoral $\frac{6}{8}$. The initial instrumentation, of clarinets, bassoons, horns and basses, suggests a serenade; this is reinforced at the entry of the solo voices by pizzicato strings.

The 'Gratias' performs a role similar to that of 'Et in terra', as a contrast to an excited passage of music. It also has a similar shape: when the chorus enters for a repeat of the tune, the harmony moves down to the subdominant, Eb. The recall of the opening theme of the movement at bar 174 suggests a new beginning in this key for the first of the 'Domine Deus' phrases; but the impulse to set the words 'Rex coelestis, pater omnipotens' with the full force of the orchestra – in the home key of D – proves too great, and the harmony rocks violently between these two poles (Ex.5.3). The conflict reaches its climax on a Bb seventh-chord, at 'omnipotens' (bars 186–8), reinforced by dynamics of triple *forte*, full organ with pedal, and (for the first time in the score) trombones:

Ex.5.3 bars 174–90, outline

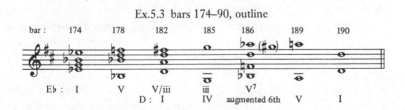

But though the resolution of the ab^2 to a♮^{2} seems to settle the issue in favour of D major, Beethoven quickly dissipates the force of the home key. The ensuing passage sounds more like the aftermath of a huge explosion, with motivic fragments assigned to various instruments and a cycle of fifths in the harmony suggesting a development section. 'Domine fili unigenite, Jesu Christe' is set as a dialogue for male and female soloists; after they join to form a four-part ensemble, the chorus answers antiphonally. This highly expressive repetition of the words 'Jesu Christe' maintains the contrast with the previous 'pater omnipotens', and at the same time propels the music rhythmically towards the next group.

The second 'Domine Deus' is a response to the first, using the 'Gloria' motif a tone higher, in F. To avoid the feeling of 'identity' between this F major and that of the ensuing 'Qui tollis', Beethoven once again reverts to the key of D, introducing the trumpets and timpani at bar 217. This time, however, the key is D *minor*, which leads smoothly – again by a cycle of fiths – towards the harmonic goal of the next section. The C major chord reached in bar 224 is strategically analogous to that in bar 117 since it, too, sets up the harmony for a section in a slower tempo; but this time C major is a plain dominant, both in origin and in destination.

Qui tollis

This section, a Larghetto of eighty bars, is the most difficult passage in the Gloria – and perhaps in the entire Mass – to understand in terms of traditional harmonic and thematic process. There is a certain symmetry in the three commands which make up the text. Each is preceded by an address, so that six elements appear in the following arrangement:

qui tollis peccata mundi	miserere nobis
qui tollis peccata mundi	suscipe deprecationem nostram
qui sedes ad dexteram Patris	miserere nobis

Apart from the use of a characteristic falling figure for both statements of 'Qui tollis', there would appear to be little correspondence between these six elements and their musical settings. However, closer examination reveals that the two-part structure of the commands is mirrored by a pairing of musical phrases. This pairing does not correspond to Classical antecedent–consequent, or question-and-answer, phrase structure: here, the first phrase of each pair seems instead to develop a terse motif or to make a strong musical gesture, while the second phrase grows from it, elaborating a more fluid idea in shorter note values.

Viewed thus as a setting of three paired phrases, the Larghetto is enhanced by text repetition. The entire line 'Qui sedes ad dexteram Patris miserere nobis' is set twice, so that three lines are in effect extended to four. This enables Beethoven to divide the music into two parts, with a caesura after bar 268 marking the end of the first two lines. As shown below, there is an extra setting for the initial 'Qui tollis' (bars 247–52) which corresponds to the orchestral introduction. This is balanced by the expansion of the final 'miserere nobis' into yet another pair of phrases (bars 292–5 and 296–309).[4]

bars	initial phrase	continuation phrase	tonality
230–7	(orch. intro.)		F – a
238–46	Qui tollis ...	miserere nobis	F – d – Bb
247–52	Qui tollis ...		Bb – d
253–68	Qui tollis ...	suscipe deprecationem nostram	D – V/D – V/Bb
269–81	Qui sedes ...	miserere nobis	Bb – V/G
282–91	Qui sedes ...	miserere nobis	V/G – F
292–309	Miserere nobis	o, miserere nobis	f♯ – V/f♯

Musical continuity consists of maintaining a clear tonal progression in the foreground, while at the same time forestalling any convincing large-scale harmonic foundation. In other words, the chord progressions are clear enough from one bar to the next, but the overall sense of direction is obscure. Phrases definitely begin and end in a key but, as shown, they do not begin and end in the same key.

One of the techniques used to promote a harmony constantly in flux is to assign the same basic chord two functions, one relating to the music just heard, the other looking ahead to the subsequent material; often a slight chromatic inflection is needed to effect the change. Thus, for instance, at the tenor solo entrance on 'suscipe' (bar 257) the harmony aims at a perfect cadence in D; but the false relation between C♯ (in the melody) and C♮ (in the bass) makes the harmony swerve towards A minor. Six bars later, another return to D is thwarted by the addition of the seventh (again C♮ in the bass), which sends the subsequent 'suscipe' along the cycle of fifths towards Bb major.

The arrival in Bb at bar 269 marks the mid-point of the Larghetto. A new theme conceived in bold rhythms appropriately sets the text 'who sits at the right [hand] of the father'. But its solidity is undermined by the timpani (in D and A) and the trumpets in D, which are forced to emphasize the thirds, not the roots, of the tonic and dominant chords of Bb.[5] The ensuing 'miserere nobis' is set in the flattened mediant major (Db), a modulation which sounds gentle after the erratic course of the previous forty bars. By an enharmonic change (C♯ for Db) the harmony moves back once again to the sharp side of the tonal circle for the repeat of 'Qui sedes' (again with trumpets and timpani, but now curiously subdued in the home key). However, a further surprise at bar 288 (Bb exchanged for Bʰ) moves the harmony once again towards the flat side during the corresponding 'miserere nobis', and comes to rest on a unison F after a perfect cadence in F major.

What now follows is the most radical disruption not only in the Larghetto, but in the entire Mass: a $^6_4$-chord of F♯ minor, with the stark fourth between C♯ and F♯ reinforced by all the brass instruments, including the trombones. Nothing in the preceding passage alerts us to this outburst, unless one's ear is sufficiently quick to pick up the unharmonized F as a possible leading-note. By way of compensation, the harmony after this point is entirely straightforward, remaining in F♯ minor and ending on the dominant. In the short orchestral postlude, this dominant is reduced to its root, C♯ , which provides the link to the 'Quoniam':

Ex.5.4 bars 306–11, outline

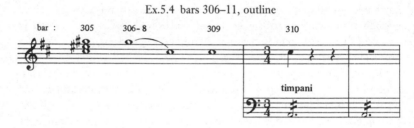

Quoniam

Traditionally, the 'Quoniam' marks the beginning of the last section of the Gloria in the Viennese mass: it is usually sufficient for the home key to be reinstated, accompanied by a return to a faster tempo. But when it is followed by a massive closing fugue, which dwarfs all that has come before, there is a danger that the music preceding the fugue will be too slight to serve effectively as an introduction.

Thus the 'Quoniam' in the *Missa solemnis* functions more like a transition between the Larghetto and the fugue. It does this successfully by not rushing into the home key too soon: the opening A major harmony (bars 312–16) is not yet a dominant, however much it may point the way to the eventual goal. And the first clear resolution to D major, at bar 327, sounds abrupt, premature in the light of the preceding C major and G major chords. Thus we have the paradoxical situation of the home key, estab-

48

lished by its tonic chord (bars 327ff.), preparing its dominant (bar 344, carried over in bar 345). The harmonic deflections in each of the concluding phrases, to B major (bars 346–7) and C major (bars 355–6) are further signs that more music will be needed to stabilize D major.

The ambiguity of the 'final' cadence in bars 359–60, with its strange inverted hairpin dynamics, is perfectly captured by the scoring: all the voices and instruments except those assigned to the bass resolve onto a short D major chord, while the bass part initiates the fugue with a semibreve D.

Thus the fugue, though required for the overall balance of the movement, is an independent element in the form. Though it may be heard as a direct response to the preceding dominant, it actually emerges from the resolution. A similar elision takes place at the end of the fugue, where the initial Gloria is brought back to end the movement.

The closing fugue

Like many of Beethoven's late fugues used to round off movements or multi-movement works, that of the Gloria is sectional and diffuse. After an initial exposition (bars 360–82), and a development in which the subject enters periodically – but rhythmically displaced (bars 383–427) – the music comes to rest on an imperfect cadence in F♯ minor. In the next section, a variety of learned devices is on offer: a solo-voice stretto of the subject, combined with a counter-melody that brings back the text 'cum sancto spiritu' in the manner of a cantus firmus (bars 428ff.), followed by a simple choral stretto (bars 440–7) overlapping with one based on augmentation of the subject (bars 445ff.). Though these points of imitation occur within a relatively short space, Beethoven keeps them distinct, first by interpolating a brief passage of harmonic instability (B, D♭, E♭, F and G minor in the space of four bars, 435–8), then by the use of solo and chorus, and finally by co-opting the trombones for the final stretto. In the build-up to the climax of the fugue, Beethoven introduces a form of inversion of the subject (beginning with tenor solo, bars 474ff.), and even a retrograde inversion of the quaver motion (alto solo, bars 484–6).

Whether the last two techniques are actually perceived in performance is doubtful: the rhythmic evenness of the fugue subject, together with its regular figuration around the pattern of rising fourths and falling thirds (a typical pattern in Beethoven's late fugues), makes it difficult to pick out precise interval successions amidst a thick texture. One could argue that the erudition displayed here conspires against a feeling of 'classical' (for example, Bachian) fugal textures: in a great wash of moving lines, the distinctness of the constituent parts is all but obliterated.

This process of textural thickening may actually be traced back to the opening bars of the fugue, where the quasi-canonic countersubject cuts in against the direction of the subject and establishes voice-exchange as an important contrapuntal principle (Ex.5.5a). The first stretto passage (bars 428ff.) is, in a sense, a development of this counterpoint, with the canonic interval of a fourth (instead of an octave) and the rhythmic displacement extended to a full bar; in three voices, this produces a pianistic texture of $^6_3$-chords (Ex.5.5b).[6] The second stretto (bars 440ff.) takes on a new motif in the high woodwind, adding voice-exchange to the $^6_3$-chords (Ex.5.5c).

Ex.5.5 (a) bars 360–1   (b) bars 430–1   (c) bar 445

Because the techniques employed in the closing fugue of the Gloria do not yield configurations which are typical of Baroque fugue, they are more compatible with its non-contrapuntal passages. Thus, for instance, the climactic unison passage at bar 488 does not sound so much like a new beginning as a continuation of the previous material. This means that a different kind of disruption – tonal, rather than contrapuntal – provides for further continuation: in the unison passage, G emerges not as the fourth scale-degree of D major (which would require its resolve to F♯) but as the root of G major and hence the fifth of C major. Instead of being treated as a neighbour to F♯ (as it is throughout the fugal exposition), it supports its own neighbour, A, in a series of plagal cadences in C major. The home key can reassert itself only by forcing its way into the harmony by brute force (see Ex.5.6b), supplanting C♮ with the leading note C♯.

The return of the opening text and music of the Gloria in the final Presto (bars 525ff.) may be seen as a purely formal device, rounding off the movement thematically while at the same time making the ending more exhilarating. In addition, it clarifies the relationship of C major to the home key, an issue previously aired in both the 'Quoniam' and the climax of the fugue. In both its appearances in the 'Quoniam' (bars 320–4 and 356–7), C major is explained as the subdominant of the subdominant, with G major as a necessary harmonic buffer. In the fugue, at bars 499–500, G major is suppressed, absent, so the move from C major back to D sounds tonally abrupt (Ex.6a): the conventional roman-number analysis ♮VII–I is an inadequate explanation. The final bars of the Presto resolve the problem of relating C major to D major, not only by restoring G major as a buffer but also by discarding the perfect cadence at the end: C major is heard as the subdominant of G, which in turn is heard as the subdominant of D (Ex.5.6b). The conflict between C♮ and C♯ no longer arises.

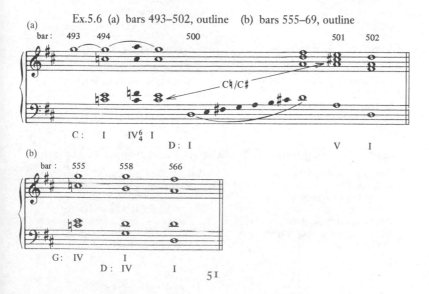

Ex.5.6 (a) bars 493–502, outline   (b) bars 555–69, outline

6

Credo

Allegro ma non troppo, C: 123 bars

Credo in unum Deum patrem omnipotentem, factorem coeli et terra, visibilium omnium et invisibilium

I believe in one God the Father almighty, creator of heaven and earth, and of all things visible and invisible.

Credo in unum Dominum Jesum Christum, filium Dei unigenitum, et ex patre natum ante omnia saecula,

I believe in one Lord Jesus Christ, the only begotten son of God, begotten of his Father before all time,

Deum de Deo, lumen de lumine, Deum verum de Deo vero, genitum non factum,
consubstantialem Patri per quem omnia facta sunt;

God of God, Light of Light, true God of true God, begotten, not made,

Being of one substance with the father, for whom all things were made;

qui propter nos homines et propter nostram salutem, descendit de coelis,

Who for us men and for our salvation came down from heaven,

Adagio, C – Andante, $\frac{3}{4}$ – Adagio espressivo: 64 bars

Et incarnatus est de Spiritu Sancto ex Maria Virgine,
Et homo factus est;
Crucifixus etiam pro nobis; sub Pontio Pilato passus et sepultus est;

And was made incarnate by the Holy Spirit from the Virgin Mary,
And was made man,
And was also crucified for us; under Pontius Pilate he suffered and was buried;

Allegro, C – Allegro molto, ¢ Allegro ma non troppo, C: 118 bars

Et resurrexit tertia die secundum scripturas;
Et ascendit in coelum;
Sedet ad dexteram Patris, et iterum venturus est cum gloria judicare vivos et mortuos, cujus regni non erit finis.

And on the third day he rose, according to the scriptures,
And ascended into heaven.
He sits at the right hand of the Father and shall come again with glory to judge the living and the dead; his reign shall have no end.

Credo in Spiritum Sanctum Dominum et vivificantem, qui ex Patre filioque procedit, qui cum patre et filio simul adoratur et conglorificatur, qui locutus est per Prophetas.

I believe in the Holy Spirit, the Lord, the giver of life, who proceeds from the Father and the Son, who is worshipped and glorified with the Father and the Son, who spoke through the prophets.

Credo in unam sanctam catholicam et apostolicam ecclesiam, confiteor unum baptisma in remissionem peccatorum, et expecto resurrectionem mortuorum,

I believe in one holy catholic and apostolic church, I acknowledge one baptism for the remission of sins, and I look forward to the resurrection of the dead,

Allegretto ma non troppo, $\frac{3}{2}$ – Allegro con moto – Grave: 167 bars

Et vitam venturi saeculi, Amen.   And to life ever after, Amen.

As with the Gloria, the structure of the text of the Credo is not congruent with the traditional layout of the music. The four statements of belief – in God the almighty Father; in Christ, son of God; in the Holy Spirit; and in a holy church – divide the text into four paragraphs with the incipits:

Credo in unum Deum
Et in unum Dominum Jesum Christum
Et in spiritum sanctum
Et in unam sanctam catholicam et apostolicam ecclesiam

Classical composers portrayed the text in a different way, as a single statement of faith focussing on that portion concerned with the story of Jesus Christ, in particular the three statements describing his time on Earth:

Et incarnatus est,
et homo factus est;
crucifixus etiam pro nobis; sub Pontio Pilato passus et sepultus est.

The meaning of the words has not been changed, but the emphasis has shifted from the doctrinal ('I believe') to the historical.

The musical gains are obvious. The line quoted above is from the middle of the Credo text and can be characterised by changes of tonality, tempo and texture. This makes some kind of ternary form a natural choice for the musical design: a contrasting central section makes for good overall symmetry (fast–slow–fast tempo, ABA tonal scheme), but the text is too short for the section to dominate the movement.

The central text is, in fact, too short to sustain a well-proportioned middle section; and this makes the setting of the Credo a far from straightforward affair. How does one organize the much longer text on either side of it, and how can one invent material that adequately expresses the three distinctive elements of the central section itself? In other words, the conventional boundary points, which seem to have been in place by the first half of the eighteenth century, offer only a first stage in coming to terms with the length of the Credo text and the variety of sentiments needed to give it expression.

An important clue to Beethoven's view of the Credo is provided by the slight change he made in the wording: the conjunction 'et' which begins the second, third and fourth statements of belief is replaced by the word 'Credo', so that each statement becomes a sentence in itself, rather than a clause in a long, unbroken text.[1] This enables Beethoven to organize the music on two levels: the traditional layout is articulated by changes in tempo and key, while the four statements of belief are underscored thematically, by the use of the four-note 'Credo, credo' motif. Further subdivisions are clarified mainly by new themes, for example, 'Consubstantialem Patri', 'Qui propter nos homines' and 'Sedet ad dexteram Patris'. Thus the Credo, like the Gloria, has a hybrid form; but here Beethoven superimposes two contrasting ways of viewing of the text, rather than giving different parts of the music a hierarchical weighting along a single scale of values.

Though a three-part design is also used in the long closing fugue and, taking into account the changes of mode, within the central section, the balance between outer sections is upset by the overall pacing: as the tempo changes in the course of the movement, the swing between fast and slow becomes ever wider until the *Allegro con moto* of the fugue is reined in to a *Grave* which marks that slowest point in the Mass reached so far.

The traditional symmetries of the Credo are further eroded by Beethoven's attention to the text, a feature which has made this movement seem a far more personal expression of belief than any of its immediate forerunners, including the Credo of the Mass in C. Though word-painting continues to be used for individual details (descending figures for 'descendit', rising ones for 'ascendit', and so on), here it actually has a substantial impact on the form of the movement. For example, the boundary between the second and third sections, instead of being marked by a single change of key and tempo, is diffused over a space of twenty bars covering three distinct tempos. Beethoven achieves this by isolating the 'Et resurrexit' from its surroundings and setting it *a cappella* in the Mixolydian mode. This exclamation, which suggests a chorus of angels proclaiming the resurrection of our Lord, is joined at both ends to music which is similarly shaped by the text: 'et sepultus est', which portrays the burial of Christ by a bass line connecting a tonic chord of D (bar 182) chromatically to the unstable interval of a fourth G–C (bar 187); and 'et ascendit in coelum', which acts as a dominant upbeat to the main body of the *Allegro molto* beginning at bar 202. Thus the visionary power with which Beethoven is able to portray the burial of Christ, the Resurrection and the Ascension has important consequences for the shape of the music.

The result of all these factors is that the notion of 'recapitulation' in the Credo is highly problematic: listeners have a choice of when to say 'here is where the third and final section begins'. Some may choose the fast tempo of 'Et resurrexit' as the beginning of the third part, some may wait until the Allegro molto *alla breve* of 'Et ascendit', or even to the harmonic resolution preceding 'Sedet ad dexteram Patris'. Others may wait until the return of the main theme ('Credo, credo' at bar 264), while still others will wait until the key of Bb finally emerges (bar 310), that is, in the closing fugue – by which time it is much too late to speak of a recapitulation in any conventional sense.

The first section (bars 1–123)

Though the Credo follows Austrian tradition in having a single tempo and key for the setting of all the text up to 'Et incarnatus', Beethoven uses a far greater number of textures than his predecessors to emphasize contrasts in the text.

An important ground for subdivision appears to be the rhythmic strength of the text. The dactyl–spondee combination of 'Deum de Deo', together with its distinctive word pattern, makes it an obvious choice for the start of something new (bar 61). Another passage singled out by Beethoven – for the first time in a Classical Credo – is 'consubstantialem Patri', whose abundance of consonants is well suited to the fugal treatment of a theme marked by repeated crotchets (bar 70). These features, taken together with the solid foundations provided by the 'Credo, credo' motif, give the first part of the movement a stately, *maestoso* character and justify its slower tempo compared to the Credo openings of earlier Classical masses.

The first sixty bars divide into two musical statements, each headed by statements of the 'Credo, credo' motif and prefaced dramatically with

IV–V–I chord-progression by the full orchestra, and conceived along the lines of antecedent plus consequent: the first ends in D minor (bar 33), the second in G minor. Yet the internal organization of the two segments owes little to the growth processes of Classical phrasing. The massive expansion of the subdominant (Eb) in bars 20–9 can of course be traced back to the initial emphasis of this chord by the orchestra, but is also justified by its effectiveness in setting up the surprise A major chord at the end of bar 30, supporting the textual opposition of 'visibilium' and 'invisibilium':

Ex.6.1 bars 28–30 (voice parts)

In the counter-statement, the subdominant is expanded again, with the progression $V^7–V^4_3/V–V^7–I$ (reckoned in Eb) in bars 51–2, while the cadence at the end is again made elusive by the successive implied tonics of C minor (bar 57) and G minor (bar 59). It is not that the chord sequences themselves are unorthodox, but that the phrase structure does not reinforce their most plausible interpretation. (The Eb progression analysed above might easily be explained as a V–I in which the dominant is expanded by a neighbouring harmony, but the phrasing makes the second pair seem like a correction of the first.)

Though the statement and counter-statement are paired chiefly on the strength of their common beginnings, and not because of any symmetrical phrase relationship, their endings are similar in the use of a sudden change of dynamics to highlight a twist in the harmony. In expressing the sense of 'things invisible', Beethoven turned the Eb chord used in bars 29–30 into a bII of D; for 'born before all ages' he goes a stage further by making Ab (bars 54–5) serve both as an extended subdominant (IV of IV of the home key) and as bII of the new harmonic goal, G minor (bar 49).

Syntactic problems continue to surface. At 'Deum de Deo', the initial G major may be heard as a secondary dominant, aiming ultimately towards the home key. But the Db chord at bar 65 comes as a shock, not only interrupting the harmony at an unexpected place but also initiating an entirely new kind of harmonic unfolding. The goal anticipated at the beginning of this subsection, a *fortissimo* climax in Bb in bar 67, remains in place; but it is not clear to the listener whether it has been reached via a cycle of fifths stretching back to bar 61 (Ex.6.2a), or whether it is more the result of linear part-writing (Ex.6.2b):

Ex.6.2 (a) bars 61–7, outline
(b) alternative reading of bars 65–7

To restore harmonic stability, Beethoven introduces a solidly based fugato for 'Consubstantialem patri' (bar 70).

The character of the next subsection, beginning at bar 90 in Db major, is determined not by text rhythms but by the meaning of the words: 'who for us human beings, and for our salvation'. This is the first passage specifically concerned with Christ's time spent on earth, and what he did for humanity.[2] The gentler orchestral texture – pizzicato strings supporting a solo flute and bassoon playing a rocking figure antiphonally – anticipates the ethereal use of the flute as symbol for the Holy Spirit in the 'Et incarnatus'. For the repeat of this text, in the home key of Bb, the rocking figure is transferred to the strings, accompanied by the wind with quiet punctuation from the trumpets and timpani. In order to round off the section as a whole, the repeat of 'descendit de coelis' (bar 112) is sung and played at full strength.[3]

The central section (bars 125–87)

As in all other Classical settings of the Credo, the *Missa solemnis* reserves the greatest intensity of musical argument for the central section. Even if the closing fugue appears to give greater emphasis to the last line of the text, it does so more by distorting the time dimension of the movement (as do all Beethoven's late fugues) than by actual concentration of musical expression. The central lines bear the greatest weight in the Credo, without dominating or unbalancing it.

It is commonplace to observe that the setting of each line expresses a different type of tonality based around D, each in accordance with the sentiments of the text:

Et incarnatus	Dorian mode	mystery of Virgin birth
Et homo factus	major	joy of Christ made man
Crucifixus	minor	suffering, death, burial

The 'Et incarnatus' is based on Beethoven's interpretation of the first, or 'Dorian', Church mode in an early nineteenth-century polyphonic context[4] and, like his use of the Lydian mode in the 'Heiliger Dankgesang' from the Quartet op. 132, is marked by a tendency to slip towards C major and a studious avoidance of Bb, except where demanded by vertical considerations.

The initial preparations (bars 124–31) give little away. The opening chord, in first inversion, has a certain 'theatrical' value, derived from eighteenth-century dramatic music: it sends the listener signals to expect a declamatory passage in D. But the two parts responsible for this recitation – tenor voice plus violas, cellos plus basses – seem forever locked in tonal conflict with one another, and the resolution to D minor never takes place. The B♮ in bar 126 might be heard as a leading-note until the bass falls to A in the next bar. The implied D minor in bars 128–9 is cancelled by the passing B♮ in the bass. In the final two bars of the tenor solo, the B♮ in the melody rules out a move to F major, C♮ a move to D minor.[5]

The fuller chords in the central phrase bring about secondary dominant chords which 'tonicize' subsidiary key areas and thus give a harmonic shape to the passage: C major (bars 132–3), G major (bar 136), and A minor (bar 141, with raised third). With these harmonies, the passage seems well directed towards its final cadence: the initial emphasis on C major, the move up to G major and the ending on A are all perfectly compatible with Dorian polyphony. The *tierce de Picardie* merely enhances the antiquated effect.

But at a larger level, the 'Et incarnatus' provides a smooth transition from Bb (as the tonic of the Credo) to D major, first by neutralizing the flats (in particular by emphasizing B♮), and then by reintroducing C♯ as a raised third, forming the leading-note to D. In other words the Dorian mode, being a negation of major/minor harmony, actually helps the listener hear A major as a framing chord for the whole passage, so that the arrival of D major in bar 144 ('Et homo factus est') is heard as its logical outcome, rather than as a surprise or contrast.

The setting of 'Et homo factus est' is harmonically straightforward: it is only the antiphony between the tenor solo and chorus and the unusual turns in the bass line that enable it to prepare for the gravity of the 'Crucifixus'. The bass refuses to make a cadence in a conventional way: its dominants either resolve upwards by step (to an interrupted cadence in bar 147) or downwards through a passing seventh to a first inversion chord (bars 149 and 152). In the end, the stepwise descent extends to a fifth in such a way that the final bass D is approached both by step (A–G–F♯–E– in bars 154–5) and by the normal cycle of (leaping) fifths (E–A–D in bars 155–6).

The purpose of a linear succession, 5–4–♯3–2–1, is of course to emphasize the D major of 'Et homo factus est', setting up the conditions for an 'explosion' in D minor at 'Crucifixus'. But rather than allowing the full force of the minor mode to make itself felt on the downbeat of bar 156, Beethoven uses a powerful unison line to erode D major gradually, one note at a time. After an ambiguous unison D, the F♮ on the second beat changes the modality from major to minor, and the B♭ on the third beat upsets the expectations of an arpeggiation of the D minor chord.

After this, the pace of destruction quickens. In the demisemiquaver that anticipates the next downbeat, the tonality of D is itself threatened, by both the C♮ in the bass (instead of an expected leading-note C♯) and the E♭ which initiates the first strand of melody. The resultant chord, C–B♭–E♭, is harmonically ambiguous, but is most likely to be heard as a supertonic of B♭, that is as II^7/VI in D minor. The collapse of the harmony is completed by the addition to this chord of a new note by the horn, sounding F♯, on the second beat of the next bar. Not only does this note contradict the suggestion of B♭, it also throws the entire orientation towards the minor in doubt, contradicting the minor third D–F♮ assigned to the horns in the first bar; indeed, the resultant chord marks a point in which tonality itself is suspended, however momentarily:

Ex.6.3 bars 154–5, harmonic outline

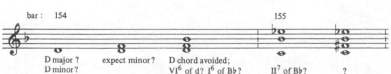

bar : 154   155

D major ?   expect minor?   D chord avoided;
D minor? VI^6 of d? I^6 of B♭? II^7 of B♭?   ?

59

It is at this climactic point in the harmony that the text of the 'Crucifixus' is introduced, with the tenor solo recitation on E♭ followed by the alto an augmented second above. The B♭ now 'resolves' to an A, simplifying the chord in the second bar to an ordinary diminished seventh.

From this point onwards, the harmony is based on more familiar procedures; but the initial thrust towards the flat side, which directs the harmony to G minor (bar 159), still has to be counter-balanced. This ultimately places greater weight upon the 'Crucifixus' within the central part of the Credo. The first step towards equilibrium around the key of D minor is taken at bar 162: the bass A is approached not by the expected route through B♮, as the harmonic sequence would require, but by way of B♭: the resultant augmented sixth-chord on B♭ makes its statutory resolution to the dominant of D.

Though the ensuing sequence on 'pro nobis' throws the harmony again off course, further stepwise movement in the bass leads to C♯ as a neighbour to D, initiating a pair of extended cadential progressions on 'passus et sepultus est' (bars 167–72 and 173–8). The gravity of the text is expressed at various levels: by the sighing figures in the slow voice-parts, by the stepwise bass (with frequent semitones), and by a persistent figure in a middle-voice for the bassoon and first violin, using anguished rhythms decorated by semitones above and below the main notes.

The long sliding fall of the bass in bar 178 reaches E♭, the root of the flattened supertonic. The next two chords (bars 179–80) may be conventionally understood as ♭II, in root position, followed by its dominant, in third inversion. What makes the progression unusual is the fall from the root of ♭II to the seventh of its dominant, setting up a conflict between the bass movement (scale-steps 1 and 4) and the chord progression it supports (I to V). The conflict is softened by the G of the cellos and basses (see Ex.6.4.a), but the unearthliness of the passage is enhanced by the immediate reinterpretation of the seventh of the chord (A♭) as an augmented sixth (G♯), making the interval of descent a diminished sixth (bracketed in Ex.6.4b).

Ex.6.4 (a)
        (b) bars 179–82, outline of part-writing

At this point the harmony leaves the safety net of D minor for the last time, slipping chromatically to C (supporting an F minor $^6_4$-chord) which is held by the sopranos and basses as the violins and double basses continue to move down from the C, ultimately coming to rest a fourth below it.[6]

The third section and closing fugue (bars 188–472)

With the resumption of a faster tempo and stable key, the third section of the Credo is set on a course which, we sense, will ultimately lead to the conclusion of the movement.

But even when the music settles into a stable motivic pattern for 'sedet ad dexteram Patris' (bars 202ff.), its tonality does not complement that of the opening of the movement, but lies a fifth higher, in F. This key, however, proves not to be a dominant but only the start of a section delicately poised between being a development and a series of loosely related episodes. The harmony reaches its remotest point at the words 'judicare vivos et mortuos' ('to judge the living and the dead'), a passage strikingly reinforced by the trombones (bar 221).

The 'judicare', which cost Beethoven as much effort as any other passage in the Mass (see, for instance, Nottebohm 1887: 155), also helps to organize the text by marking the end of a subsection. The setting of 'cujus regni' resumes the orchestra's 'sedet' motif, in D major, which struggles towards a Bb major chord to mark the arrival of the original tempo of the Credo. The resolution to Bb would seem a desirable goal, the return of the 'Credo, credo' motif at Tempo I. But we must remember that the movement had originally begun off the tonic, and so the arrival at Bb merely initiates a IV–V–I progression in F major. The movement must continue for some time in F (and its companion tonality, D) before regaining the

home key at the start of the closing fugue. The stages in which the home
key is forestalled are summarized below:

bar	text	chord	remarks
188	et resurrexit	G major	Mixolydian mode serving as dominant of C; Crucifixus extended beyond D minor (bars 183–7) to improve connection
194	et ascendit	C major	actually dominant of F major
202	sedet ad dexteram Patris	F major	begins long delay of B♭ major; D major used as companion key
264	(Credo, credo)	B♭ major	B♭ major superimposed over unison ending on D; B♭ still remains IV of F, with D as companion key
289	(et expecto)	F major	begins dominant preparation of B♭
310	(et vitam)	B♭ major	long awaited resolution on B♭

The closing fugue, on the words 'Et vitam venturi saeculi, amen', is a contrapuntal *tour de force* which brings a long movement to a close in much the same way as the Gloria. (It is tempting to suggest that these colossal constructions were partly a response to Prince Esterházy's criticism of the earlier Mass in C for not containing a proper fugue.) The Credo fugue (outlined in Table 3) is more unified – and ultimately more satisfying – since it contains fewer sections, develops a relatively simple idea (essentially a subject in minims for 'Et vitam venturi saeculi', accompanied by a countersubject in crotchets for 'Amen'), and is basically assigned to the full chorus: the soloists contribute only to the 'Amen' of the final *Grave*. Like many late-period fugues, it is a compendium of contrapuntal device: double fugue, inversion of the subject, stretto, and rhythmic diminution. Bekker was right to link it spiritually to the finale of the 'Hammerklavier' Sonata and the *Große Fuge*; the three fugues ought also to be grouped for their sheer technical accomplishments.

Table 3. *Structure of the closing fugue of the Credo, showing the entries of fugue subjects*
S–soprano   A–alto   T–tenor   B–bass
entrances identified by implied key
all entries in Part 2 are rhythmically diminuted

Part 1 (bars 306–72)	Part 2 (bars 373–438)	
Introduction (306–9) [see Ex.6.6a]	Introduction (373–8)	
Exposition 1 (310–27)	Exposition (379–87)	
S 310 Bb	T 379 Bb	
A 314 F	A 381 F	
T 318 Bb	S 383 Bb	
B 322 F	B 385 F	
Episode (328–33)	Episode (388–98)	
A 328 Bb (2 bars only)	S 388 D (=V/g)	
S 329 F	T 389 G (=V/c)	
Exposition 2 (334–46)	A 390 c	
A 334 Eb	B 391 c	
B 338 Ab (inverted)	S 393 Bb (incomplete)	
T 342 Db	A 394 Eb	
Episode (347–57)	Cadence preparation (399–438)	
S 347 Db (inverted)	dominant pedal	399–406
B 349 Db	[cf. bars 306–9 and	
A 353 Eb (2 bars only)	Ex.6.6a]	
S 354 - (1 bar only)	plagal cadences	407–10
Reprise (357–68)	concluding chords	410–12
S 357 Bb	[see Ex.6.6c]	
T 364 F (incomplete)	dominant pedal	413–16
B 365 Bb	plagal cadences	420–4
Concluding chords (369–72)	concluding chords	424–7
[see Ex.6.6b]	cadential phrase	433–8
	Part 3 (Coda: bars 439–72)	
	soloist's entry	439–42
	(without chorus)	
	2nd solo phrase	443–50
	(chorus: 'amen')	
	3rd solo phrase	451–63
	(chorus: 'et vitam venturi	
	saeculi, amen')	
	orchestral ending	464–72

The Credo fugue also contains what Beethoven might conservatively have described as 'alcune licenze', as he did for the 'Hammerklavier' fugue. The shape of the subject and the countersubject is usually fixed for four bars (see Ex.6.5: note the two voice-exchanges in bar 3, which bind their rhythmically independent threads), but the last bar is often modified to accommodate the entries of new voices or the direction of the harmony:

Ex.6.5 bars 310–14, subject and countersubject of closing fugue

From an outline of its structure (see Table 3), one can see that there is quite a bit of symmetry and recall, which might easily be overlooked in view of the tremendous momentum it generates in the course of its 163 bars.[7]

The first part (cautiously marked *Allegretto ma non troppo*) is in ternary form, prefaced by a cycle-of-fifths progression for the woodwind, supported by a dominant pedal in the horns and resolving to the tonic after four bars (Ex.6.6a). After a full exposition, and a middle section which inverts the subject and explores the flatter regions of the tonal circle (reaching Eb minor and Gb major in bars 353–6), Beethoven recapitulates the fugue subject in the home key before moving to a striking series of root-position major triads to set up the key of D major (Ex.6.6b).

The second part likewise begins with an orchestral introduction, setting the normal version and rhythmic diminution of the subject against each other (and, at the same time, wiping the modulation to D). It follows with a full exposition, using the diminished subject and a new countersubject, in quavers. This material is developed in flat keys less remote from the tonic (C minor, E♭ major) before returning to the tonic by way of a dominant pedal (bars 399–406). Here Beethoven expands the chord progression with which he had introduced the fugue, and continues with a series of plagal cadences (foreshadowing the end of the movement); the passage is capped by another striking group of root-position major chords (Ex.6.6c). Bars 413–27 repeat this process – dominant pedal supporting the cycle of fifths, plagal cadences, root-position chords – to ensure that the huge Handelian full close in the final tempo, *Grave*, is adequately prepared by non-fugal textures.

Ex.6.6 (a) bars 306–9, outline   (b) bars 369–71, outline
          (c) bars 410–12 (424–6), outline

The last section (the 'Coda' in Table 3) focusses on the single word, 'Amen'. It begins with a short, quasi *a cappella* passage for the soloists, leading to a passage of vocal duets accompanied quietly by the chorus. A more florid variation of this phrase (bars 451ff.) leads naturally to a series of rising scale-figures, taken up by the strings and woodwind (bars 457–60 and 464–7), before the final, plagal cadence.

7

Sanctus

Adagio: mit Andacht, $\frac{2}{4}$ – Allegro pesante, C – Presto, $\frac{3}{4}$, 78 bars

Sanctus, sanctus, sanctus,	Holy, holy, holy,
Dominus Deus Sabaoth!	Lord God of Sabaoth!
Pleni sunt caeli et terra	Heaven and earth are full
gloria tua.	of thy Glory.
Osanna in excelsis!	Hosanna in the highest!

Praeludium: sostenuto ma non troppo, $\frac{6}{8}$, 32 bars

Andante molto cantabile e non troppo mosso, $\frac{12}{8}$, 124 bars

Benedictus qui venit	Blessed is he who comes
in nomine Domini.	in the name of the Lord.
Osanna in excelsis!	Hosanna in the highest!

Early sketches for the movement

Although a full-scale study of the genesis of the *Missa solemnis* is beyond the scope of this book, I shall attempt here to outline the progress of early work on the Sanctus and to relate this to the final version. For a list of the manuscript sources for the Mass, see Table 1.

Beethoven appears to have made relatively few sketches for the Sanctus; those which survive are scattered among several manuscripts covering a wide time-span, which makes it difficult to piece together its genesis. What they do show, however, is that its overall form changed radically during the composition of the Mass: more radically than that of any other movement.

Probably the earliest idea for the Sanctus was entered in pencil in Beethoven's handwritten copy of the Mass text (T):

Ex.7.1 sketch in T, p. 5.

[time signature ambiguous]

de - us sab - a - oth   sanct   dom - i - nus de - us   sabaoth

The character of this music is very similar to that of the brass chorus, which acts as a punctuation mark between the sung passages (bars 9–12, 19–20, 27–9). What is of course striking is that it was originally conceived as the main theme, in other words as the musical setting of the text 'Sanctus, sanctus'. The sketch cannot be dated precisely; but its position in T suggests that it preceded the main work in the sketchbooks. It may have been entered soon after Beethoven began work on the Mass in the spring of 1819.

The first sketchbook entries date from December 1819; they follow a substantial block of Credo sketches in the 'Wittgenstein' sketchbook (S1). Beethoven marked page 81 of this manuscript in large letters 'Sanc' ('Sanctus'), rather like a title-page; this is typical of the way he marked the beginning of sustained work on a section of music. Here the four-note opening motif begins a tone lower than in the final version:

Ex.7.2 sketch in S1, p. 81, staves 1–4

The goal, however, is the same: the dominant chord of A major, supporting a recitation of the first line of text. The entire section was to be about twenty-five to thirty bars. There are as yet no indications of a brass hymn used to punctuate the vocal phrases. In other words, Beethoven conceived two ways of beginning the Sanctus: with a chorale-like idea (Ex. 7.1), and with a four-note motif used as a point of imitation (Ex. 7.2). In the end he put these ideas together, making one the 'ritornello' for the other.

The 'Pleni' was sketched in F major in S1, with rapid semiquavers in a fugal texture representing the fullness of God's glory in heaven and on earth:

Ex.7.3 sketch in **S1**, p. 81, staves 7–10

This only lasted about twenty bars in $\frac{2}{4}$ time, and was to be followed immediately by the Osanna in the same tempo, without a break to indicate a new section:

Ex.7.4 sketch in **S1**, p. 82, staves 1, 4

A sketch for an instrumental introduction to the Benedictus in C major (S1, p. 82) shows that Beethoven was thinking of using solo instruments at an early stage. Here a solo cello (marked 'violone') and, most probably, a solo violin weave embellished arpeggios around a chorus of four horns:

69

Ex.7.5 sketch in S1, p. 82, staves 11–14

The remaining Mass sketches in S1 contain only a few jottings for the Sanctus, of which the remark (p. 87):

Benedictus kann auch fröhlich sejn   The Benedictus can also be cheerful.
Gesegnet   gelobet sej der der   Blessed [praised] be he who

suggests that Beethoven may have known Haydn's *Harmoniemesse*.

The parallel pocket sketchbook (P2) gives the same opening for the Sanctus, a 'Pleni' in F major (now in common time, with the semiquaver passage work assigned to the flutes), and an 'Osanna' in F major. (A later entry in P2 gives the 'Osanna' in D.) The sketches for the Benedictus look extremely tentative, and bear no indication of solo instrumental scoring. A few months later, however, in the summer of 1821, Beethoven was still searching for a suitable instrumental timbre for the introduction to the Benedictus. In a relatively large gathering of unstitched leaves (G7), concerned mainly with the end of Credo, he wrote down three possibilities:

Benedictus Eingang   Introduction to the Benedictus
mit Horn Violoncello violin   with horn, cello and violin
nach art eines prelud   in the manner of a prelude

Benedictus   Benedictus
Harpa violino so[lo]   harp and violin solo
oder orge[l]   or organ

Benedictus 2 clarinetten	Benedictus: 2 clarinets
oder 1 clarinette u Eine viola	or one clarinet and one viola
violino solo / violoncello solo	solo violin, solo cello

The first two sets of remarks are accompanied by very rudamentary sketches, suggesting the key of C major.

Accompanying the third set, however, are three pages of jottings that give a clearer picture of the shape of the movement. It opens with the same figure as in S1 and P2, but now a fourth higher, that is, a third higher than in the final version:

Ex7.6 sketch in **G7**, p. 30 (of reconstructed gathering), staves 9–15

The passage still ends on the dominant of D, and leads once more to a vigorous 'Pleni' in F major, still in common time with the semiquaver passage-work assigned to the flutes. The 'Osanna' follows in F major, immediately after the 'Pleni', and closes in a plagal cadence:

Ex.7.7 sketch in **G7**, p. 29 (of reconstructed gathering), staves 15–16

The Benedictus is now in A major, with important solo material mapped
out for the violin, cello, horns and clarinets. The remarks 'einmal im 1ten
Theil' and 'einmal im 2ten Theil ('once in the first part', 'once in the
second part') show that Beethoven conceived the movement in two 'parts',
in other words a movement in sonata form.

Ex.7.8 sketches in **G7**, p. 31 (of reconstructed gathering), staves 6–15

After these sketches, there is no record of work on the first part of the movement: the general shape of the 'Sanctus' suddenly emerges on a loose sketch-leaf (see Plate 1). No sketches survive for the D major 'Pleni' and 'Osanna' fugatos, apart from some very late corrections in G11 and G12, dating from 1822.

Virtually all subsequent work on the movement is concentrated on the Benedictus in the early months of 1821, in the last twenty pages of S2 and in its contemporary pocket sketchbook, P4. These sketches are too numerous and substantial to describe here, and deserve a special study of their own.

Sanctus–Pleni–Osanna

The Sanctus is the only movement to begin without a clear sense of harmonic direction. The opening four-note figure in the bassoon and double basses, B–C#–A–D, is tonally ambiguous; its subsequent transpositions in the cello and viola suggest a constant sharpening of the tonality, from D to A to E by way of their dominants; a tentative resolution on a second-inversion E minor chord (bar 4) signals a move to the flat side. This is halted by an equally tentative resolution to D major by way of a first-inversion dominant, introducing the brass choir.

The brass choir appears to settle the question of tonality: its solemn music pushes firmly, though not forcefully, towards a cadence in D major, but this is subverted by an interrupted cadence onto B minor. This cadence ties in, of

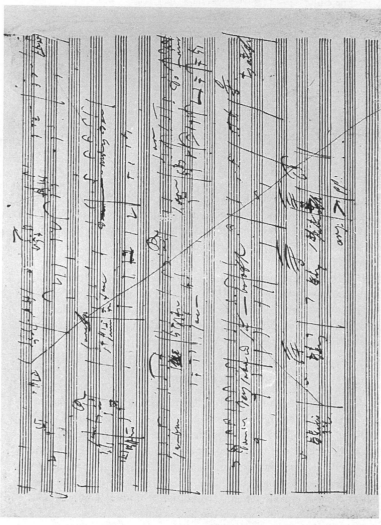

Plate 1: Deutsche Staatsbibliothek Berlin, mus. ms. autogr. Artaria 180, p.114: draft of the opening of the Sanctus.

course, with the tonal ambiguity at the beginning: the basses begin again with the note B, and the orchestral introduction is repeated – with modifications – as the voice-parts enter with their own point of imitation, forming a simple counterpoint to the opening motif.

The 'Sanctus' thus begins in the manner of an operatic *scena*, the orchestral introduction being recycled for the entry of the voices in bar 12. This section is, naturally, expanded; in place of an aimlessly roving harmony, Beethoven constructs a regular (eight-bar) antecedent phrase whose arrival on the dominant is marked by a short ritornello (bars 19–20).

The consequent phrase starts a tone lower, on A in the basses, and, after further harmonic ambiguity, subverts an expected A minor ending in bar 26 to make a perfect cadence in B minor. The brass chorus duly returns, and converts B minor to a submediant by aiming for a perfect cadence in D major. This cadence is held back by a homophonic recitation of the opening line of text over a first-inversion A major triad that is gradually expanded to include the seventh and minor ninth above, and the root – provided by the timpani.

The dominant ninth-chord resolves onto the beginning of the 'Pleni'. This resolution marks one of the most interesting ambiguities in Beethoven's harmony. There can be no doubt about it being a V–I progression in D; but is it meant to be heard as a succession of chords in root position (with the timpani alone providing the bass line), or are the timpani meant to be heard simply as colouring, the true bass-line being C♯ (supporting a diminished seventh) to F♯?

In the 'Pleni', each voice enters a third lower than the previous one; the illusion of fugato is preserved by the quasi 'tonal answers' suggested by the reformed arpeggiations: of 6–4 chords in bars 34 and 38, 6–3 chords in bars 36 and 40:

Ex.7.9

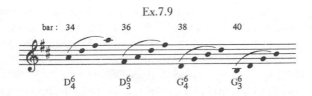

As a companion piece to the 'Pleni', the first 'Osanna' is also cast as a fugal exposition in D major, this time as a genuine fugue with tonal answers in the alto and bass parts. As in traditional fugal scoring, the woodwinds and strings double the voice parts in register, starting from the oboes and working downwards. The string parts play a decorated version of the subject; the resulting heterophonic texture gives the six *sforzandi* in the first two bars extra pungency, thus strengthening the impact of the underlying counterpoint.

The one irregularity in the fugal texture occurs midway through the third (tenor) fugal entry, where the soprano drops out for six bars. This enables Beethoven to bring the sopranos back for a fifth fugal entry (following two 'false' entries, in the alto and soprano) and thus to end the section with the voices in their highest registers; appropriately, the flutes are withheld until this final entry.

The final cadence is the most impressive event in the 'Osanna': the soprano's high g^2, an upper boundary-note in the fugue subject, is now forced upwards against its will, so to speak (as the seventh above the dominant), and resolves to a^2.

Praeludium and Benedictus

If the Benedictus seems the most extended, most leisurely, perhaps the most self-conscious number in the *Missa solemnis*, this is entirely in keeping with the Austrian mass tradition. Not only is it intended to contrast with the vivacious settings of the surrounding texts, 'Pleni' and 'Osanna', it also represents the point of greatest contrast in the entire Mass setting, the point at which the austerity of choral polyphony yields to the sensuousness of instrumental music.

Because these conditions usually result in an extended piece, usually in a slow tempo, and in a key which represents a 'relaxation' from the tonic (most suitably, the subdominant), the problem arises: how does the Benedictus work in relation to the Sanctus as a whole? Its formal independence, its tonal position and its restfulness are all at odds with its position in the text, as an interior element placed between two statements of 'Osanna in excelsis'; it is difficult for two short, quick outer sections framing a long, slow middle section to make a satisfactory form.

The solution to this problem is to make the Benedictus not an interior element in the movement but its goal. For this innovation we must credit Haydn. In four of his late masses, the fourth movement ends in the tonality and mood of the Benedictus, the second 'Osanna' being absorbed into the musical fabric as unobtrusively as possible: these are the *Missa in tempore belli*, the *Heiligmesse*, the *Theresienmesse* and the *Schöpfungsmesse*. It was Haydn who first recognized that, the longer the Benedictus, the less a repeat of the first 'Osanna' could be tolerated on musical grounds: thus the late-Classical Sanctus becomes one of the earliest testing-grounds of what is sometimes called 'progressive tonality', where movements begin and end in different keys.[1]

Where the *Missa solemnis* differs from Haydn's examples is in its rejection of the hard edge between the first part of the movement and the Benedictus; in other words, Beethoven is attempting to break down the concept of 'movement' as an integral, unified musical construction with a recognizable design. This can be seen most obviously by his conceiving a 'Praeludium', an interlude written in imitation of an organ improvisation (though not calling upon the organist to realize it); it forges a link between the two parts of the movement which are otherwise worlds apart. It is easy to overlook, however, that throughout the movement the concept of a 'home key' is constantly undermined, for example, in the very opening bars which grope towards a D major tonic, and in the 'Pleni', which loses its grip on the tonic at the end. Nor is the Benedictus itself based on solid G major foundations: Beethoven consistently subverts the points of arrival in this part of the movement, allowing them to open up new areas of instability.

This instability is already forecast in the Praeludium which (despite its key signature of one sharp) takes its starting-point of D major from the end of the 'Osanna', loses its footing early on, and makes frequent attempts to lift itself back onto the D major track – at bar 85 and bar 95 (with dominant seventh chords), and once more at bars 100–1 (with a diminished seventh) – before resigning itself to G major in bar 104. The absence of a well-defined theme in these thirty-two bars (the Praeludium sounds like a fantasia on fourth-species counterpoint) enables Beethoven to drop the level of tonality from D to G without calling any attention to the process; the Benedictus enters like music from another world, its subdominant relation to that of the rest of the Mass only dimly perceived.

The arrangement of the movement is so unusual that it is difficult to determine where the Benedictus actually begins. If the Praeludium is its introduction, then it begins in bar 110 with the first-inversion chord assigned to the solo violin and flutes, that musical ray of light which announces the imminent appearance of Christ at the altar (Kirkendale 1970: 688). But this chord merely marks the beginning of a descending phrase which prepares the first statement of the main theme, in bar 119; and even this theme is part of a catalogue of themes which acts like a ritornello before the entry of the solo voices in bar 134.

The presence of a solo violin throughout the Benedictus might suggest an organization of musical materials in the manner of a concerto. In fact, it is not the violin but the solo voices which take on a concertante role by shaping the music in the exposition and recapitulation. The solo violin is the agent of change from the antique austerity of the earlier parts of the movement to the more 'modern' sound of the last part. In the Benedictus itself, it either adds an extra dimension to the orchestral accompaniment, as a secondary obbligato part (albeit made prominent by its high register), or it is used as an extension to the range of the solo singers (for example, the dialogue with the soprano in bars 146–51). The chorus is treated, in effect, as part of the orchestra: this is seen already in the bass incantation (bars 115–17), and more tellingly in the recitations of 'in nomine Domini' in bars 156–9 and 196–9.

But it would be wrong to say that the Benedictus actually follows a Classical concerto plan. The overall design of the movement, outlined in Table 4, has little in common with that of concerto first-movement form, apart from the opening catalogue of themes (which I call a ritornello) and sections which are roughly approximate to an exposition and a recapitulation.

It is the concluding theme of the exposition, identified as (f) in Table 4, which blows the Benedictus off the concerto course. This is the point where a second ritornello would be used to consolidate the dominant tonality (that is, D major, bars 142–55). But Beethoven not only halts the drive to the dominant by the interrupted cadence at bar 156 (a technique previously used in the Violin Concerto), but lets the tonality fall back to its original level, G major. Thus the position of the second ritornello and the development section of the Classical concerto movement are reversed. The passage of harmonic transition – the 'development' (bars 159–66) – precedes the second ritornello (167–75), instead of following on from it.

The result of this reversal of view is that the second ritornello has a preparatory role, rather than a culminating one. Instead of consolidating the end of the exposition in the dominant, it introduces the 'recapitulation' in the subdominant, making C major the contrasting tonality. In this way, the overall tonal plan of the Benedictus is a large-scale I–IV–I progression, instead of I–V–I.

In addition to the 'inverted' tonal plan and the unconventional use of

Table 4. *Structure of the Benedictus*

First part

110–18 Introduction (instrumental trio descending from g^3–d^3–b^2)

First ritornello (G major)
(a) 119–21 principal theme: solo violin
(b) 122–3 clarinet and bassoon quartet
(c) 124–30 secondary theme: solo violin beginning on V^7
(d) 131–3 cadence theme: descending scale in solo violin

Exposition (G major to D major)
(a) 134–9 principal theme: alto and bass solo in canon
(b) 140–1 modulation: clarinet and bassoon quartet
(a) 142–5 principal theme: soprano and tenor solo in canon
(c) 146–8 secondary theme: soprano solo and solo violin
(d') 148–55 cadence theme: soprano solo, with florid solo violin
(e) 156–8 'in nomine' chorus: VI–♯IV^7–IV after interrupted cadence

First transition (G major to C major)
(f) 159–66 'qui venit' chorus, with florid solo violin

Second part

Second ritornello (C major)
(a) 167–9 principal theme; solo violin
(b) 170–1 clarinet and bassoon quartet
(c) 172–5 secondary theme: with hint of Introduction

Recapitulation (C major to G major)
(a') 176–9 principal theme in C major: tenor solo
(a') 180–2 principal theme in G major: bass solo
(c') 183–5 secondary theme, cadenza-like: soprano, alto solos
(c) 186–7 secondary theme: alto solo and solo violin
(d') 188–95 cadence theme: alto solo, with soprano solo and solo violin
(e) 196–8 'in nomine' chorus: VI–♯IV^7–IV after interrupted cadence

Second transition (C major to G major)
(f) 199–211 'qui venit' assigned to solo voices
(b) 212–13 clarinet and bassoon quartet as transition to 'Osanna'

Third part ('structural coda': G major)

(g) 214–22 'Osanna in excelsis' fugue: subject derived from (b)
(c) 223–7 'thematic coda': secondary theme
(b) 228–34 theme taken in turn by solo violin, chorus, clarinet

instrumental and vocal soloists, the Benedictus departs from the concerto tradition in its deployment of theme. Classical concertos tend to be generous in their deployment of themes; the Benedictus, however, is thematically parsimonious, recycling its material in a more symphonic manner. The main theme, for instance, is heard first as a solo melody (bars 199–22), then as a canonic duet for two solo voices (Ex. 7.10a) and finally as a development of the canonic setting as a single line (Ex. 7.10b).

Ex.7.10 (a) bars 134–5   (b) bars 176–8

In addition, Beethoven allows a single theme to take on a variety of functions. Theme (b), for woodwind quartet, is used first of all to link material in the same key (bar 122), to effect a modulation to the dominant (bar 140), or even to serve as a conclusion to a section (bars 212–14). The procedure is entirely in keeping with a 'symphonic' style, but it further distances this part of the movement from the genre of concerto.

The second 'Osanna'

It was relatively late in the sketches for the Benedictus (on one of the last pages of S2) that Beethoven noted that the second 'Osanna' might follow on from the Benedictus without a change of tempo or a return to the material of the first 'Osanna':

osanna selbiges tempo des bened.   Osanna in the same tempo as the Benedictus

This comment is of great significance for the way we view Beethoven's understanding of the Mass's structure. First of all, it shows that he wanted to proceed along a line different from that pursued – unsuccessfully – in the Mass in C. Secondly, it suggests that working out the second 'Osanna' in the tempo of the Benedictus was not a procedure that was taken for granted as an option in settings of the mass around 1820; or, if it was, it suggests that Beethoven was more isolated from current practice than has been commonly supposed. In accepting Beethoven as an exponent of an 'Austrian mass tradition', it is easy to suppose that he was familiar with a representative selection of the music of his predecessors in the genre, including some of the four late Haydn masses whose second 'Osanna' settings are absorbed into the ending of the Benedictus. The above remark in S2 shows, on the contrary, that Beethoven either recognized only at a late stage how Haydn's example could help him solve the problem of the second 'Osanna', or that he rediscovered the solution for himself without recourse to Haydn's scores.

But Beethoven went one stage further than Haydn. Though dissatisfied with the *da capo* 'Osanna', he nevertheless felt unable, on liturgical grounds, to dismiss this element of the text by denying it a thematic profile of its own. The solution was to make the second 'Osanna' a section in its own right, as a coda to the movement. Its traditional role of contrast could be realized by a change of texture; and the obvious choice of texture is, of course, fugue.

The orchestration supports the new texture from bar 214 onwards, a Baroque type of scoring in which instruments double one of the choral parts in accordance with their range. Moreover, instruments banished from the Benedictus because they would threaten its peaceful, quasi-pastoral mood, are readmitted for the fugal 'Osanna': the contrabassoon (doubling the bass line) and the oboes (doubling the altos and sopranos).

And yet the point of grafting the second 'Osanna' onto the Benedictus would be lost if a material connection between them were not attempted. Once again, the slender theme (b) is pressed into service, joining the second transition to the coda and providing the actual theme of the new 'Osanna'. The theme, by being preceded with an upbeat D, not only fits the rhythm of the word '*Osan*na' but also gains that harmonic solidity required by a fugue subject. Thus Beethoven ends one section of the movement (bars 212–13) and begins another (bars 214–15) with the same material. The miracle of the Benedictus is its musical economy.

The delicate balance between textural diversity, on the one hand, and thematic relationship, on the other, is further reflected by the details of the Coda. After the 'Osanna' fugato climaxes on a first-inversion dominant seventh (bar 222), it is time for the Benedictus to be recalled once more, both in texture (solo violin, accompanied by the clarinet and bassoon quartet) and theme. (I call this the 'thematic coda' of the Benedictus because the solo violin returns to play its most characteristic music, theme (c).) After the violin trill on high f$\sharp^3$, the 'Osanna' and Benedictus strands are fused into a single phrase, with theme (b) played or sung alternatively by the violin, choral tenors and clarinet as the movement eases gently towards a plagal cadence.

8

Agnus Dei

Adagio, C, 95 bars

Agnus Dei, qui tollis peccata mundi, miserere nobis.	Lamb of God, who takes away the sins of the world, have mercy upon us.

Allegretto vivace, $\frac{6}{8}$ – Allegro assai, C – Tempo I – Presto, ₵ – Tempo I; 339 bars

Dona nobis pacem.	Give us peace.

The principal tasks of the final movement of an eighteenth-century Austrian mass are, from an expressive point of view, to make an effective contrast between the phrases 'qui tollis peccata mundi, miserere nobis' and 'dona nobis pacem'; and, structurally, to make a satisfying conclusion to the work as a whole. For a mass conceived in symphonic terms, where tonal coherence, thematic integrity and good proportions are essential, the Agnus Dei must tie together any loose ends resulting from the conflict between musical structure and text expression. For instance, when the Benedictus is conceived as a quasi-independent piece (not followed by a recapitulatory 'Osanna') and ends outside the home key, the Agnus has to bring the tonality back to the home key.

This does not usually entail a drastic effort from the composer. In his *Theresienmesse*, Haydn ends the Benedictus in G major, absorbing the repetition of 'Osanna in excelsis'; the Agnus Dei begins with an introduction in the parallel key of G minor, which moves on to its relative key, B♭ major, the home key of the Mass. A similar procedure can be seen in the *Missa solemnis* (Ex.8.1): Beethoven uses third-related keys in such a way that adjacent tonics have two notes in common, so that modulation becomes a more linear process, rather than one determined by standard chord progression:

Ex.8.1

Tradition kept a tight rein on the setting of the text, and to a large extent on the form of the movement, until the early nineteenth century. The 'Agnus' was always in a slow tempo, and in a key that contrasted either in modality or tonality with the main key of the movement. For the 'Dona' the metre was changed and the tempo was faster; the tonality returned to the home key. Thus the movement took on the two-part form of slow introduction plus *allegro*.[1]

Originally, the parts of the text concerned with mercy and with peace were not placed in direct opposition to one another, but were rather part of a three-line scheme:

Agnus Dei, qui tollis peccata mundi, miserere nobis.
Agnus Dei, qui tollis peccata mundi, miserere nobis.
Agnus Dei, qui tollis peccata mundi, dona nobis pacem.

In the Middle Ages and Renaissance, this required three separate movements. For the Baroque 'cantata mass', two independent numbers were sufficient: a setting of the first line (for example, as a solo aria), and one of 'Dona nobis pacem' (as a final chorus). Classical composers observed the repetition in the text by making the 'Agnus' cover the first two-and-a-half lines and end on a dominant chord, as a preparation to the 'Dona' in the home key. (Many of Haydn's masses follow this scheme literally: the *Missa in tempore belli* departs from it only slightly by including a quiet 'Dona' as part of the long dominant at the end of the slow introduction.)

If Classical composers thought generally in symphonic terms when considering problems of musical unity, that is, if their experience with instrumental music in the sonata style determined much of the shaping of a setting of some established 'standard text' such as the Mass Ordinary, then the obvious solution to the form of the Agnus Dei would have been slow introduction plus sonata-allegro. They had only to ensure that the overall result sounded like the ending of a work, not an intellectually weighty opening movement.

The settings of the Agnus Dei in Haydn's late masses avoid the character of symphonic first movements by eschewing thematic links between the two parts, and by minimizing the sonata arguments in the 'Dona'. In the 'Nelson' Mass, for example, the forty-one-bar 'Agnus', an *adagio* in G, dwarfs the seventy-seven *allegro vivace* bars of the 'Dona', a sonata form in miniature.

Beethoven, however, had conceived the earlier movements of the *Missa solemnis* on a far grander scale than Haydn's masses and devoted more time to expressing the meaning of the words; thus he could not have allowed the simple arrangement of a slow introduction plus cursory sonata movement to serve as its conclusion. As one so often finds in his 'heroic' designs (for example, the Third and Fifth symphonies, the 'Waldstein' and 'Appassionate' sonatas), the expanded dimensions are followed through to the last movement. The trend to shift the weight of a multi-movement piece to the finale is even stronger in his late music: for the *Missa solemnis*, a quick exit number would have been unsatisfactory.

There existed a traditional solution to the 'finale problem', namely to re-use the music of the Kyrie in the 'Dona nobis pacem' (Haydn's *Nikolaimesse*, Mozart's 'Coronation' Mass K.317, and Diabelli's popular 'Pastoral' Mass) or to quote it at the end (Beethoven's Mass in C), thereby making the mass setting a truly cyclic one. But if symmetrical procedures of this sort had become outmoded by 1820, Beethoven's sensitivity to the music–historical tradition – of which he now felt himself a part – would have prompted him at least to hint at earlier thematic material. This is where Riezler's 'germinal motive' becomes a useful concept: but rather than generating a vast number of themes in the mass as a way of guaranteeing motivic unity (as Riezler saw it), this figure merely suggests thematic relationships at various points and on different levels.

The 'Agnus'

The structure of the text also determined the structure of the 'Agnus' of Classical mass settings. The words 'miserere nobis' are a response to 'Agnus Dei, qui tollis peccata mundi', and this is readily translated into an antecedent phrase (ending on the dominant) followed by a consequent phrase (ending on the tonic, sometimes in a new key). This pattern would be repeated (in a different key), and usually followed by a third, incomplete statement leading to the 'Dona'.

In the *Missa solemnis*, however, Beethoven allowed the ternary design to be played out completely, with three full settings of the plea ending with 'miserere nobis'. This gives greater rigidity to the music, which in this respect is akin to the ternary Kyrie. The architectural quality is further underscored by the symmetrical phrase lengths, and by the use of the subdominant as contrasting key:

Bar	Statement	Key	'Agnus Dei'	'qui tollis...'	'miserere nobis'
1	I	b	8 bars	8 bars	10 bars
27	II	e	8 bars	8 bars	11 bars, overlapping with:
53	III	b	8 bars	8 bars	3 (interpolation) + 10 bars
82	continuation	→e			4 + 6 bars
92	transition	→D	4 bars		

What distinguishes this design from earlier Classical settings, and justifies the severity of the whole, is the subdivision of each antecedent phrase into two parts: 'Agnus Dei' plus 'qui tollis peccata mundi'. Each part ends on the dominant, but the second amplifies the imperfect cadence in the first and thus demands a more extensive continuation on 'miserere nobis'. The twenty-six bars needed for just one statement of the text in the *Missa solemnis* already begins to approach the length of an entire Classical 'Agnus'. So Beethoven's ninety-five-bar 'Agnus' has the proportions of a movement in its own right, while not relinquishing its role as an introduction to the 'Dona'.

The anguish of the text is expressed by the darkness of B minor, Beethoven's 'schwarzer Tonart', as he once described it in a sketchbook (Nottebohm 1887: 326), which is conveyed chiefly by wind instruments in close position in a low register.[2] The opening chorale for bassoons and horns is followed by the entry of the bass solo in bar 5, and the four-part male choir in bar 14; higher voices and instruments are introduced in stages, and not until the second and third statements. The atmosphere of desolation is emphasized by the additional weight given to the subdominant. At the highest level, the 'Agnus' expands a plagal progression from B minor to E minor and back. In each phrase-component of the three statements of the text, the subdominant (or its close relation, the II_5^6–chord) is given prominence.

In the one irregularity of the formal design, the interpolation at bars 69–71, the harmony shifts suddenly to the flattened supertonic. Here the aural dominant-to-tonic relation between the 'German sixth-chord' and the chord of the flattened second, already articulated in the 'Crucifixus' (Credo, bars 179–80), sets up the progression of bII–I by way of linear 'slippage', that is, without an intervening dominant (see Ex.8.2). The continuation of the third section in the home key (bars 82–91) also

Ex.8.2 bars 69–72, outline

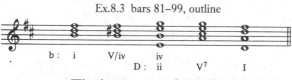

b :   V$^4_2$/♮II   ♮II^6 ♮II   i
      (German 6th)

calls for special attention. It would have been normal to use the dominant
to heighten the tension here, or to move towards the dominant of D major
to prepare the 'Dona'. The tenacity of B minor, underscored by appoggia-
turas in the accompaniment at crotchet and quaver levels, pushes the music
to the brink: the B minor chord must ultimately give way. Yet a persistent
minor chord cannot yield in a conventional tonal manner, by resolving as a
dominant, since it lacks the major third. The way out of the dilemma is to
raise the third so that it can behave as a dominant: it resolves to E minor, a
key already stressed in the 'Agnus', which now functions as a pivot for the
'Dona' in D:

Ex.8.3 bars 81–99, outline

b :   i   V/iv   iv
           D : ii   V^7 I

The beginning of the 'Dona'

What sets Beethoven's 'Dona' apart from earlier settings is that it continues
to be based on contrast. The opening phrase, instead of suggesting that an
ending is nearly in sight (as in Haydn and Mozart), merely pulls the music
gently onto a D major track, without suggesting the future course of events
or even the nature of the struggle to come.

This is, of course, the struggle between War and Peace, one that is
amply documented by verbal remarks in the sketchbooks and autograph
score (Drabkin 1991a).[3] Viewed in technical terms, this struggle is articulated by an orchestra designed to play in D major (with clarinets in A, all
four horns in D) opposed by a 'military' component comprising two Bb
trumpets and timpani in Bb and F. We do not learn this until after the
entire 'Agnus' and the exposition of the 'Dona' themes have been heard.[4]
The tonal opposition between I (D major) and bVI (Bb) is played out twice
in the movement and helps to clarify its form by dividing a broad sonata
design roughly into three parts: exposition, development plus recapitulation, and coda.

In the 'Dona', the sonata principle can be seen at work mainly in the presentation and recapitulation of themes, rather than their development. This is another sign of what Adorno meant when he said that the *Missa solemnis* lacks Beethoven's personal signature (1964: 150): the Mass as a whole, especially in its more obvious sonata structures in the Benedictus and 'Dona', does not show the composer's usual determination to conquer a single theme by persistently breaking down its melodic, harmonic and rhythmic components.

If thematic development plays only a small role here, it must be compensated for either by brevity (which the length of the 'Agnus' and the programme of the movement as a whole has ruled out), or by a multiplicity of themes. Table 5 shows the exposition divided into seven distinct sections, only one of which – the transition from the home key area to the dominant – can be described as working out an earlier musical idea. (The themes themselves are written out in Ex.8.4.)

As a general rule, the shorter a text, the more its musical setting tends towards an 'abstract', that is, a musically based form: when the text is just three words long, verbal sentence structure is not of much help to musical structure, nor is it easy to imagine the highlighting of a key word (in this case, 'pacem').

To make the text appear longer, Beethoven took the unprecedented step of basing entire themes on single words, 'dona' or 'pacem': in this way, for example, the 'second subject' divides easily into a group of themes, at the same time fulfilling the sense of the words. For in Classical sonata form the second subject generally marks a point of repose, an area of tonal stability (in the new key) and regular phrasing (a tune based on regular four-bar phrases). This is the musical analogue to Peace, and it is appropriately conveyed here by a theme (d) which sets the single word 'pacem' in long note values and fills regular phrase-patterns; around this the violins and woodwind weave a delicate counterpoint in staccato quavers. This is followed, for sake of contrast, by a fugato (e) whose built-in contrapuntal animation perfectly satisfies the demands of an imperative verb, 'dona'. The closing subject reaffirms the demand for Peace with a simple I–IV–V progression (f^1) or repeated tonic chords (f^2).

Two other, related devices for extension are employed: the recall of text from the 'Agnus', and the composing of sections of varying length for orchestra alone. The orchestral music marks the ends of major sections of the form; taken together with the music based on the text borrowed from the 'Agnus', they form the two 'interruptions' (see Table 5) which divide the movement into three parts. By recalling the full text of the Agnus Dei, Beethoven reminds us that its last three words should not be thought of in isolation but are actually part of a longer sentence in the liturgy: 'Agnus Dei, qui tollis peccata mundi, dona nobis pacem.' The text is distributed as follows:

bars 174-89:
Alto: Agnus Dei, qui tollis peccata mundi
Tenor: Agnus Dei,   miserere nobis
Chorus: miserere nobis!
Soprano: Agnus Dei,
                                                   → dona nobis pacem

and bars 345–53, following the longest orchestral interlude:

Chorus: Agnus Dei,   dona pacem
Soprano: dona pacem

All three extension devices help Beethoven make 'pacem' the focal point of the text. The word 'pacem' is given greatest emphasis in the music in the dominant (bars 131–63), and hence consolidates our perception of sonata form. The absence of text, together with the recollection of words set earlier in the movement, gives us the two disturbances of Peace (at bars 164ff. and 266ff.) which mark the end of the exposition and recapitulation, respectively. Sonata form can further be understood in relation to the prayer for Peace: the exposition responds to the plea for mercy conveyed by the 'Agnus', the end of the development and the recapitulation to the sounds of War in bars 164–90.

The multiplicity of theme in the Agnus Dei reminds one of another Classical form: the concerto. The opposition of soloists and chorus (and of singing and playing) lends itself well to antiphonal writing and phrase construction from small thematic building-blocks, rather than to development of a small number of ideas. The obvious models for this procedure are the first movements of Classical concertos, especially the piano concertos of Mozart which Beethoven so greatly admired.[5]

The challenge of Classical concerto composition lies in creating a logical succession of themes. Where the role of motivic development is severely curtailed, the task of creating a convincing series of events becomes more of a challenge. Each 'new' theme must be different from the one that has come before, yet at the same time must be perceived as a sensible continuation. In Example 8.4, I have shown how melodic and rhythmic traits are shared between two or more themes by bracketing similar passages and numbering the traits for easy identification:

Table 5. *Sonata form in the 'Dona nobis pacem'*

First part

Exposition of first group
(a)	98–107	main theme	D
(b)	107–22	'pacem' fugato	D
(c¹)	123–6	*a cappella* theme (chorus)	D

Transition
(c²)	127–30	brief development of descending sixth	D→A

Exposition of second group
(d)	131–8	'pacem' in long note values	A
(e)	139–47	'dona' fugato	A
(f¹)	148–55	'pacem' closing theme	A
(f²)	156–63	'pacem' concluding chords	A

Second part

First interruption and development
164–89	'War' interlude	B♭→
190–211	development of (a)	→D

Recapitulation
(c¹)	212–15	*a cappella* theme (soloists)	D→D⁷
(c³)	216–40	lengthy development of descending sixth	G–D
(d)	241–8	'pacem' theme in long note values	D
(e)	249–57	'dona' fugato	D
(f¹)	258–65	'pacem' closing theme, lacking ending	D

Second interruption
266–325	orchestral double fugato based on (b)	D–B♭
326–53	new sounds of War	→B♭¹
354–8	transition based on beginning of (a)	→D

Further recapitulation
359–74	(a) sung by soloists (incomplete) and chorus	D

Third part

Coda (absorbing more recapitulation)
374–434	various subsections, including:	D

> (b) 'pacem' fugato (374–8, 380–4)
> (f²) 'pacem' concluding chords (384–92)
> (c¹) *a cappella* theme (accompanied) (402–5, and so on)
> quiet timpani solos (406–9, 412–15)

Ex.8.4 themes of the 'Dona nobis pacem' (see Table 5) and their shared melodic traits
(a) bars 98–107 (b) bars 107–10 (c^1) bars 123–6 (c^2) bars 127–8
(d) bars 131–4 (e) bars 139–41 (f^1) bars 148–51 (f^2) bars 156–60

1   melodic fall 5–4–3, supported by V–I harmony
2   falling sixth
3   ♩. ♩. + ♩. ♩ ♪ rhythm, or vice versa
4   turn figure (3–2–1–2 or 3–4–3–2), or neighbour-note figure (5–6–5–5)
    in even note-values
5   repeated notes in even note-values

The 'War' interruptions and their consequences

The Peace of the second group is interrupted in bar 164 by the sounds of War. This interruption proved to be the most difficult part of the 'Dona' for Beethoven to compose. It initially took the form of a march: the sketchbooks of 1821 and 1822 show that some half dozen march tunes, in a wide variety of keys, were tried out here. It was also among the last passages in the *Missa solemnis* to be worked out in its final form: the length of the trumpet fanfares was adjusted several times, and the scurrying string parts in bars 168–70 were probably the last entries in the autograph score apart from dynamics and articulation.

The fanfares have nothing in common with the themes of the 'Dona'; and the voices respond to this music by taking the form of recitative, further ensuring that this section maintains a foreign character. Only with the plea for Peace at bar 190 do we return to earlier thematic material: the opening of theme (a) resurfaces, and is developed in such a way that the tonality gradually circles back to the home key. For a traditional sonata form movement, this would not be a long development section; considered together with the War music, however, it puts considerable distance between the end of the exposition and the reprise of the *a cappella* theme (c¹) at bars 212–15.

The next section (bars 216–40), labelled (c³) in Table 5, has been linked by many writers to the 'Hallelujah Chorus' from Handel's *Messiah*. Some regard it as an unconscious reference to a work Beethoven is known to have admired and once considered re-orchestrating. Others call it an intentional quotation, one which uses the 'English' quality of Handelian oratorio to convey the spirit of peace brought to Europe by the Duke of Wellington's campaigns (Kirkendale 1970: 696), or the order in human affairs brought about by the establishment of parliamentary democracy in Great Britain.

No reference to the Hallelujah Chorus has ever been found in the sketchbooks, despite the numerous extracts from *Messiah*. The sketches show rather that the passage in question is derived from the transition in the exposition, theme (c¹), its relation to the *a cappella* theme reinforced by Beethoven's description of it as a '6tengang', a progression of descending sixths (Drabkin 1991a). Of course, the fact that the G major episode is much longer than its counterpart in the exposition (a mere four bars), and that trombones now support the voice-parts, makes its function ambiguous. On the one hand, it strives after the status of an independent section in G major (this is where Kirkendale's idea of a rondo comes in (1970:696)); on the other hand, it functions like a secondary development section separating the first- and second-group themes in the recapitulation.

The themes of the second group are recapitulated in order, but the final chord of (f¹) is omitted, allowing the second orchestral interlude to intrude (bar 266). This section of the piece has inspired a variety of interpretations, the most plausible of which is that it represents the disturbance of that 'inner peace' to which the subtitle of the 'Dona' refers; the point is put persuasively by Kirkendale (1970: 696–8). Thematically it is closely allied to theme (b) in the exposition, the double fugue subject deriving from the opening of the duet for choral sopranos and basses:

Ex.8.5

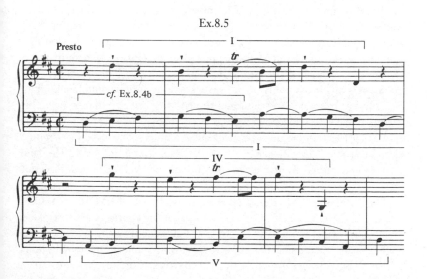

(While the sketchbooks show that it was always Beethoven's intention to have a fast fugato towards the end of the 'Dona', the autograph manuscript shows that the change of metre from $\frac{6}{8}$ to *alla breve* was a last-minute decision, made after several bars of the section were written down in the score.)

One of the most unusual features of Example 8.5 is the harmonic relation between the fugue subject and its answer. The upper line of the subject is answered a fourth higher, the lower line a fourth lower (bar 268), so that the original interval of an octave, on the tonic, is answered by a seventh on the dominant. This striking twist on the concept of tonal answer is unrepeated in the fugato, which soon degenerates into a freer contrapuntal play for the orchestra in a concertante style.

As the harmony spins towards B♭, the sounds of War return with much louder and more terrifying noises from the trumpets and timpani, only to yield once more to the power of prayer. Theme (a) functions as the bridge once again (bar 359), but this time begins squarely in D major and so can bring the music to a provisional close in bar 374.

The Coda

The one remaining problem is the organization of the coda, which must continue in the key of D. A triumphant conclusion, with a prominent fanfare based on the first part of (a), was tried out in the sketches in 1821. This would have entailed changing the key of the trumpets from B♭ to D, and the idea was given up in favour of a gradual *decrescendo*, both in actual dynamics and in thematic profile (Drabkin 1991a). The solution to the problem is ingenious. Only one of several themes not recapitulated before bar 266 has been given a triumphal return after bar 359: theme (a). This means that the section perceived as a coda (bars 374 to the end of the movement) actually includes a considerable amount of necessary recapitulation (see Table 5). Beethoven begins with theme (b), sung in bars 374–7 and 380–4, and played by the orchestra (in the manner of a 'reminiscence theme') in bars 394–401.

The newness of the coda is ensured by a change of texture: instead of making the 'pacem' fugato a subdued affair for the chorus in a low register, Beethoven marks the music *espressivo* and assigns it to the soloists in the higher octave. In the final moments of the work, theme (c^1), originally sung *a cappella* but now performed by the full chorus and orchestra, reappears in three places as a means of punctuating the various orchestral ideas of the coda. In the first recurrence, Beethoven develops the previous theme (b) in such a way that (c^1) follows on even more smoothly from it than at the beginning of the 'Dona' (compare bars 122–3 with bars 401–2). In the next two recurrences, the characteristic bass note B♮ (bars 405 and 411) jars against the solo timpani B♭ used to represent the dying sounds of War;[6] the tonal conflict is delicately intensified by the augmented second between the timpani B♭ and another note in the bass, C♯ (bars 409–10 and 415–16).

Finally the 'pacem' theme (**d**) is gently put to rest by the horns; the response of the strings leads effortlessly into (**c**^{1}), at bar 425. In the *Missa solemnis*, especially in the last two movements, Beethoven strives after a more natural musical expression, disarming the listener accustomed to hearing him struggling violently with materials or painstakingly working out an intellectual argument. The melting of theme (**d**) into (**c**^{1}), in effect the last event in the 'Dona', provides a final reminder that great effects in music need not always sound hard-won.

9

Concluding thoughts

Connections between the movements

It is generally agreed that the music of Beethoven's maturity is among the most highly organized in the repertory of the eighteenth and nineteenth centuries, and that the analysis of any work – choral or instrumental – should take into account not only the structure of the individual movements but also the connections between them. Music theory, however, is conventionally concerned with dynamic processes – chord progressions, melodic motion, musical form as movement between regions of instability and stability – and is ill-equipped *as a theory* to determine the conditions under which one can sensibly draw connections between distant points, for example on the basis of thematically similar material. Moreover, a thematic relationship between, say, two or more movements of a symphony is no guarantee that the symphony is well-composed; more importantly, the absence of such relationships cannot in itself be regarded as a shortcoming of its composition.

Nevertheless, analysts are bound to return to the question: what makes these particular movements belong together, as parts of a single work and not merely as a series of discrete pieces? The question may properly be asked of any work whose individual parts – whether songs of a cycle, movements of a sonata, or numbers of an opera – are intended to be performed in succession; indeed it must, ultimately, be asked of such works.

The question is also applicable to a setting of the Mass Ordinary, but not exactly for the same reasons nor to the same extent; the history of the genre and the context in which mass settings are to be performed affect the answer. The Renaissance composers established a precedent for thematic integration, for example by the use of a *cantus firmus* or 'motto' running through each of the movements, or by the technique of paraphrasing a song or motet ('parody mass'). Beethoven, who was conscious of the mass tradition of his own time and whose interest in earlier music greatly increased in later years, would not have failed to rely on historical values (however he may have understood them) when approaching a task with which he had little previous experience (or success). On the other hand, the kind of motivic integrity demanded of a symphony would not necessarily have been transferred to the genre of sacred music, for two reasons: firstly, traditional sacred music was more contrapuntal by nature, at times dominated by fugal textures; and secondly, the individual movements of a Mass – unlike those of a symphony – were normally destined to become adornments for a religious service, rather than to be considered as parts of an artistic entity. I say normally, for the composition history of Beethoven's *Missa solemnis* offers up an interesting paradox which is, I believe, crucial for an assessment of the way it works as a whole.

When Beethoven conceived the idea of a mass to celebrate the coronation of Rudolph as Archbishop of Olmütz in the spring of 1819, he was thinking of music for a religious service in which only two of the five parts (the Kyrie and Gloria) would be performed consecutively. But by February 1823, at the point of completing the work, he was advertising its performance as an oratorio, that is, as a concert work in which all five movements would be heard in succession. This was how the work was first performed, evidently to great acclaim, by the St Petersburg Philharmonic Society in April 1824 (Fischmann 1970: 278–9).

Now one should always be wary of Beethoven's pronouncements about his own work, and all the more so about a choral work which required special pleading to attract a large market. We may, for instance, discount his assurances to Carl Friedrich Zelter of the Berlin *Singverein* that the Mass could easily be sung *a cappella* ('with slight alterations it could even be performed by voices alone') as an utterly insincere piece of sales-talk (Anderson 1961: 996). But the idea of the Mass as oratorio rings true for the dimensions of the work in its final form. Lasting over an hour, it would have dwarfed any religious service it may have been intended to enhance. It should also be noted, peripherally, that throughout the last decade of his life, Beethoven wanted to write either a second opera on a serious subject or a large-scale oratorio, and that his friends had set great store by a collaboration on the oratorio *Der Sieg des Kreuzes* with Josef Karl Bernhard. Thus the *Missa solemnis* can in a sense be viewed as Beethoven's fulfilment of one artistic mission (the composition of a mature oratorio) by redesigning another project (a coronation mass) which he had not completed in time for the occasion it was meant to serve.[1]

If connections between the movements are to be purposeful, and not merely decorative (thematic similarities that happen to strike the ear, or eye), then we could start by looking at how one movement leads to the next, to see if the ends of movements are in some ways incomplete, and if the beginnings of subsequent movements pick up the loose musical threads just heard.

Riezler's 'germinal motive' (see Ex.1.1) is a useful starting-point, since it provides the open-ended material from which the Kyrie grows. The melodic shape F♯–B–A–G–F♯ is more than an ascending fourth which is then filled in: it signifies melodic incompletion, the failure of a descending figure to reach its goal-note: D in the key of D major. The end of the Kyrie not only elaborates this figure (see Ex.4.5) but also distils it to the point at which only the two notes of the tonic triad, A and F♯, remain. The Gloria then provides closure by melodically completing the tonic triad in bars 3–4:

Ex.9.1

Significantly, the join between the Kyrie and Gloria is made before the new movement takes off: the opening four bars of the Gloria form an orchestral introduction, and stand apart from the pair of six-bar phrases which sets the full chorus in motion and establishes a balance between tonic and dominant.

The join between Kyrie and Gloria is, of course, liturgically correct: since they are performed consecutively in the mass service, the idea of one as a prelude to the other enhances the relationship between them. Between the Gloria and Credo, which are not liturgically contiguous, Beethoven needed to create contrast rather than continuity. The Credo is the only movement of the Mass which begins and ends outside the tonic and, being the longest, is in effect the centrepiece of the work. Its opening IV–V progression in Bb major, supporting g^2–f^2, may be heard as a response to the plagal cadence at the end of the Gloria supporting the final notes of the 'germinal motive', g^2–$f♯^2$:

Ex.9.2

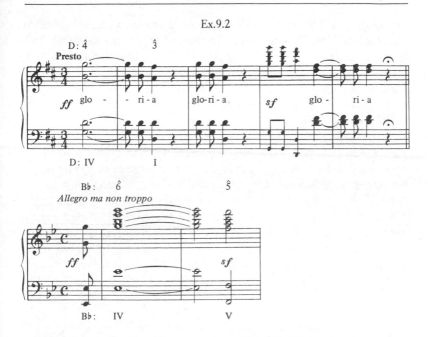

Here, of course, there is no question of the Gloria seeming incomplete and thus in need of rescue by the opening of the next movement: its plagal cadence caps a section which is both liturgically gratuitous (a reprise of the opening 'Gloria in excelsis Deo') and musically unnecessary after the excesses of the movement's closing fugue. But it provides the perfect set-up for the Credo, whose task must somehow be to break fresh ground, by sweeping away the after-image of D major with its powerful opening chords. Again, the connection is made with the help of music outside the body of the movement to which it belongs: the two chords are entirely introductory, indeed Beethoven conceived them only at a relatively late stage of the composition, well after the main sketching of the Credo.

After the Credo, the Mass seems to begin anew. The opening bars of the Sanctus recapture the devotional mood of the Kyrie (with the expression-mark *mit Andacht*, 'with devotion' reappearing) as they grope for a tonality and a phrase structure; the 'Pleni' marks their arrival. Thus the 'Sanctus' and 'Pleni', seen from an expressive point of view, recapitulate the Kyrie and Gloria.

Between the Benedictus and the Agnus Dei, there is once more a feeling of harmonic 'progression'. The B minor tonality, with which the final movement opens, not only provides a setting for its anguished text but also puts the music back on course for an ending in the home key of D. The harmonic progression from G major to B minor (illustrated in Ex.8.1) is articulated in the treble once again by the end of the 'germinal motive': the Benedictus ends on G, the 'Agnus' begins on F♯.

This pair not only forecasts the melodic prominence which F♯ will gain in the themes of the 'Dona', but also points the way towards another kind of thematic link in the Mass which Beethoven may have forged on historical principles. As explained earlier, there was a tradition in Austria of repeating the music of the Kyrie in the 'Dona', to round off the mass as a whole and make it truly cyclic; Beethoven's Mass in C nods in the same direction by quoting the first eleven bars of the Kyrie at the very end of the 'Dona'. In the *Missa solemnis* this practice is preserved by subtle thematic links between the outer movements: the *a cappella* theme of the 'Dona' transforms the 'germinal motive' into a much more complex melody while retaining its scalar descent from b^1 to $f\sharp^1$. It presents the crucial pair, G–F♯, on two registral levels:

Ex.9.3 (a) Kyrie, bars 3–7, outline (cf. Ex.1.1)
        (b) Agnus, bars 123–6, outline (cf. Ex. 8.4c)

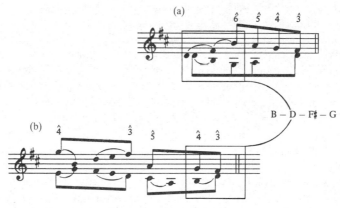

And it is this theme which is treated as a 'reminiscence theme' at the end, so that it ties together not only the 'Dona' but also the Mass as a whole.

Orchestration

Although the *Missa solemnis* is not a symphony, it shares several features with that genre. It comprises a number of movements of which the majority (including the first and last) are in the home key. It is scored for a large ensemble, but not a vast one: the voices and organ are the only performing forces additional to the symphony orchestra of around 1820. Given Beethoven's experiences as a symphonist, one would expect the composition of the *Missa solemnis* to bear some relation to that of the symphonies in terms of disposition of the orchestra.

One could go so far as to suggest that, by the end of the eighteenth century, settings of the Mass Ordinary had been so strongly influenced by principles adopted in instrumental music – sonata form, symphonic scoring – that they began to attain the status of abstract designs, rather than responses to the message of a text. That is, although the text was still the starting-point of the composition, a set of conventions had given rise to a familiar five-movement form which was analogous to that of the four-movement symphony (or string quartet), or the three-movement sonata. (This seems to have been the basis of E. T. A. Hoffmann's criticism of Haydn's church music.)

Two factors, however, argue against this viewpoint. First, the *Missa solemnis*, despite being the work of a composer noted almost exclusively for his instrumental music, remains a setting of a text; it must therefore be viewed as an expression of that text, regardless of Beethoven's reputation as a craftsman of 'abstract' or 'absolute' musical designs. Secondly, the Mass was Beethoven's first large-scale work with orchestra after 1812. There can be no question of his having forgotten the art of instrumentation: the 1814 revision of *Fidelio* and the overtures of opp.113, 115 and 117 kept him in practice as an orchestrator. But the development of his style between 1812 and 1819 was, inevitably, to affect the style of his orchestral writing once he returned to the medium. The words 'From the heart – may it return – to the heart' seem more applicable to the sonatas and the song cycle dating from these years of personal withdrawal. If we are to interpret them as a qualifying mark on the score of the *Missa solemnis*, then Beethoven seems to be saying to us: 'I have written a grand Mass – an oratorio – for large performing forces; yet it is no less deeply felt than any of the more intimate pieces I have written since 1812.'

Beethoven's techniques of orchestration widened during the composition of the Mass. From a basically Classical approach to scoring, he expanded in two directions: backwards, towards the Baroque technique of using instruments registrally, and forwards towards the Romantic idea of instrumental tone-painting. In the fugues, for instance, he gives up the Classical, hierarchical system of orchestration whereby the strings dominate the texture, the woodwind have an antiphonal role, the horns reinforce the tonality, and the remaining brass and timpani articulate the dynamic contrasts. The technique itself is not new: what distinguishes the *Missa solemnis* from earlier Classical examples (especially Beethoven's own Mass in C) is the sheer quantity of fugal writing. In addition to the massive closing fugues of the Gloria and Credo, fugal textures spring out in many places, and with increasing frequency in the course of the work. In this respect, the Mass confirms the sound-world imagined by E. T. A. Hoffmann to be the true and proper medium for 'new choral music'.

Where the Mass does not acknowledge the archaic aesthetic of sacred music, it often moves far beyond the Classical set-up of the orchestra by exploring the pictorial or symbolic value of individual, or groups of, instruments. The best-known examples of this are the flute at 'Et incarnatus', as a musical representation of the Holy Spirit in the form of a dove; the brass chorus in the 'Sanctus', as 'tower music' representing the singing of angels (Kirkendale 1970: 686); the solo violin in the Benedictus, as the presence of Christ on the altar; the trumpets and timpani in the 'Dona', as the elements of War; the trombones in various passages in the work, as the symbol of the power of God (for example, at 'omnipotens' in the Gloria and 'judicare' in the Credo).

That Beethoven's orchestration takes him backwards and forwards in time, so to speak, when special circumstances require it does not mean that the rest of the Mass is orchestrated conventionally. Only the Kyrie preserves a generous measure of Classicism in its use of instruments: this is appropriate because its text is too short to suggest imagery or to accommodate a fugue. Thus, for instance, the same theme will be scored differently in the wind if it is played in different keys. The theme at bar 50 in the first 'Kyrie' (Ex.9.4a) is assigned to the first oboe (doubled by horn) because this instrument was the most important woodwind instrument in the Classical orchestra; in this passage the remaining brass and timpani underscore the tonic, D major. In the second 'Kyrie', where the theme first reappears at bar 165 in G major, it is reassigned to the flute (doubled by clarinets) and virtually all of the brass support falls away (Ex.9.4b).

The return to D major two bars later is marked by a return to the original orchestration, exactly as one would expect in an eighteenth-century score.

Elsewhere, things are not so tidy. 'Qui sedes' in the Gloria (bars 269–72), for example, uses a powerful I–V progression in Bb major, with strong dotted rhythms (see Ex.9.5). The trumpets and timpani join in; but because they have been tuned for a movement in D major, they are capable of playing only the third of the tonic and dominant. The scoring is contrary to Classical convention.

This may have been intentional: the imposing image of Christ seated 'at the right hand of the Father', conveyed by the harsh voicing of the chords, then contrasts with the gentler, more fluid plea for mercy which follows. Nevertheless, it is characteristic of Beethoven increasingly to assign notes to instruments merely because they are capable of playing them and because a certain volume (or type) of sound is required, instead of choosing an ensemble that is more naturally suited to the characteristics of the instruments and the tonality of the passage.

In the absence of a theory of instrumentation (comparable to a theory of tonality or rhythm) it is not easy to define what a 'natural' or even conventional scoring consists of. Certainly, the ways of scoring symphonic music common in the late eighteenth-century would not have dominated orchestral music of the early nineteenth century to the same degree: the spread of virtuoso solo playing to wind instruments, coupled with major improvements in their design and manufacture, gradually worked its way into orchestral scoring. Beethoven's symphonies, though often seen as a high-point during the first hundred years of the genre, can – from the viewpoint of instrumentation – also be regarded as transitional works, leading from the well-ordered hierarchical scoring of eighteenth-century Classicism (culminating in Mozart) to the emancipation of individual instrumental sonority by the Romantics. The *Missa solemnis* is part of that transitional process; and because of the way in which Beethoven set its highly suggestive text, it represents a significant move towards a Romantic ideal.

The *Missa solemnis* as programmatic music

Although programme music is not exclusively the province of the orchestra, an ensemble of varied instruments with a wide dynamic range is an obvious advantage to its realization. There can be no doubt of Beethoven's intention to have certain instrumental sounds represent musically what the

Ex.9.4 (a) Kyrie, bars 49–53

Ex.9.4 (b) Kyrie, bars 164–8

Ex. 9.5 Gloria, bars 269–72

words express; this is borne out of the verbal remarks in the sketchbooks. The question is: do they add up to a piece of music which is programmatic, that is, one whose structure is governed by the words and what they stand for?

There can be no easy answer to this question. On the one hand, the overall shape of the *Missa solemnis* is similar to that of many earlier Classical masses. On the other hand, it casts its expressive net much wider: where the attention paid by earlier composers to details in the text results more in subtle nuancing, Beethoven appears to make these details the focus of his setting, and to ensure that the shape of the music can accommodate these details. In other words, it is the response to the text that accounts for the greater range.

Even the return to a particular key, which would normally be recognized as a unifying event in a Classical orchestral setting because of the recurrence of recognizable timbres, does not necessarily have structural significance in the *Missa solemnis*. The two B minor sections, for instance, use the orchestra in contrasting ways: the 'Christe' aiming at a more homogeneous sound (in a quasi-Baroque manner); the 'Agnus' using choruses of wind instruments and the strings antiphonally.

Another instance of tonal reprise is the 'Et homo factus est' in D major. It is sometimes remarked that this passage helps unify the Mass by recapitulating its home key, thus linking the one movement not in D major – the Credo – to the rest of the work. Yet the instruments most obviously capable of making a connection to a 'home key', namely the trumpets and timpani, are missing here because they have been tuned to a different tonic, B♭. It might then make more sense to regard D major at 'Et homo factus est' as a temporary side-tracking of the quasi-minor Dorian mode at 'Et incarnatus', allowing the true D minor of the 'Crucifixus' to hit the listener with full force. In other words, D major in the Credo is an internal element of the tonality, with a limited structural range. The failure of the scoring to keep a tight rein on the musical fabric makes it easier for us to view the Mass as the expression of one sentiment after another.

Against this view, one may argue that Beethoven avoids giving the impression of an entirely 'foreground' setting by protracting one phrase of the text in each movement, thus imposing a structure upon it. The gigantic fugal finales of the Gloria and Credo are the most obvious examples of this. Of course, we cannot go so far as to assert that each of these movements is in the form of a huge prelude and fugue; yet one can say that the immensity of the fugues dwarfs the ideas presented earlier, frustrating the listener's attempts to retain a vivid recollection of earlier pictorial events. The image of Christ seated at the right hand of the Father is quite striking in the 'Qui tollis' section of the Gloria, as is that of the Holy Spirit in the 'Et incarnatus' of the Credo; yet both will have long faded from the memory by the time the intricately constructed closing fugues have run their course.

The same holds true of the Sanctus, and further explains the reason for avoiding a reprise of the first 'Osanna'. The long Benedictus, in a modified version of sonata form, functions in the same way as the closing fugues in the Gloria and Credo by consolidating a movement which has otherwise consisted only of fragments.

Structural and programmatic techniques meet on equal terms in the 'Dona nobis pacem'. Here, it may be recalled, it would not normally have been necessary for Beethoven to write a long finale, since tradition had kept the 'Dona' to a modest length and the preceding section was based on a single sentiment, the plea for mercy ('miserere nobis'). But having expanded the central movements of the Mass, Beethoven felt it necessary to find a way of giving the Agnus the necessary weight to round off the work as a whole. Thus the programmatic element, the war-mongering of the trumpets and timpani in a foreign key, is incorporated for the first time into the *concluding* section of the movement: and the length and complexity of the 'Dona' (another modified sonata form) becomes the result of the programme rather than of an attempt to counter-balance any musical symbolism presented earlier.

In this respect the Agnus, which was conceived in its entirety only after the shape of the other movements was more or less fixed, in 1821, is the most original part of the Mass. In the 'Dona', the programmatic and structural elements of the work cannot be separated from one another: the earlier struggle between music and text-expression for a dominating role is now resolved in favour of a perfect balance between the two: the meaning with which the composer endows the words 'Dona nobis pacem' determines the form which his finale takes. That Beethoven was able to realize this plan successfully, yet still remain faithful to the basic design of the late eighteenth-century Austrian mass, is one of the – many – miracles of his last years.

Notes

1 Critical perspectives

1 Partly because of the shortage of religious music of the highest quality by Beethoven, writers have had to seek an explanation of his understanding of God outside the musical sources, for example in his letters and especially in the *Tagebuch* (diary) written during some of the gloomiest years of his life, 1812–18. For a transcription of the *Tagebuch*, see Solomon 1982; for an illuminating discussion of Beethoven's attitude to religion, see Solomon 1983.
2 Kirkendale, however, thought that in the Benedictus Beethoven was 'quite unambiguously associated with the aria "He shall feed His flock"' (1970: 690).
3 The conversation-book entries relating to the Mass had already been studied systematically some time before by Luigi Magnani (1962). Neither Winter nor Kirkendale appear to have known about his work, despite its relevance for their research.
4 For a more up-to-date survey of the loose pocket leaves, see Drabkin 1991a.
5 Georgiades 1977; Lester 1970; Virneisel 1966. Each of these studies is concerned with only a few details in the Mass; collectively they shed little light on the later stages of its genesis.

2 Composition, performance and publication history

1 Beethoven biographies have perpetuated the idea, first put forward by Anton Schindler, that Beethoven began teaching Rudolph in 1803–4 and wrote the piano solo part of the Triple Concerto (1804) for him (Schindler 1966: 140). But the earliest documentary evidence of contact between the two men is Beethoven's dedication to Rudolph of the Fourth Piano Concerto (1808). From the surviving evidence, it now seems more plausible to date their relationship from around that time (Brandenburg 1988: 141).
2 Schindler reported, in the second edition of his biography (1860), that Beethoven had begun the Mass in the autumn of 1818 (Schindler 1966: 228). This date is now generally discredited, being at odds both with the evidence in the sources and with the account given in the first edition (1840) of Schindler's biography.
3 One way Beethoven sought to reassure Simrock and Peters that they had not, after all, been betrayed was to claim that he was working on a second Mass and actually intended to write a third one, and that they would soon be receiving one of the three works. These letters have led some biographers to suggest that at least one Mass may have been left unfinished at the time of his death. But the sketchbooks give barely more than some verbal ideas about other settings, such as a 'Klavier-Messe' (a mass with keyboard accompaniment) or a 'new Mass with wind and organ accompaniment only'; the actual composition of these works could only have been wishful thinking on Beethoven's part, and the sketchbook entries represent no more than a half-hearted attempt to unburden a guilty conscience.

3 Preliminaries to the analysis

1 The only evidence which I have encountered of Beethoven's familiarity with Vienna's churches is a remark on a leaf of sketches dating from the spring of 1820 (it was torn from the end of the 'Wittgenstein' Sketchbook):

Nb in den augustinen mit diesen zwei chören mi[t]ten oben eine Messe oder te deum laudamus.

NB: in the [church of the] Augustinians with its two choirs above and in the middle, a Mass or Te Deum laudamus.

Here, the architecture of a church apparently suggested to him the composition of a sacred work with two choirs (though the idea never came to fruition).

2 I believe that not only the 'Pleni' and 'Osanna' but also the opening 'Sanctus' section should be performed by the full chorus. In Austrian mass settings of the period, the 'Sanctus' was almost always assigned to the chorus, the solo parts entering only in the Benedictus. This was Haydn's procedure in all his later masses (apart from a very small modification in the *Missa in tempore belli*), and Beethoven's in the Mass in C. Had Beethoven decided on something quite different for the Missa solemnis, would he not have made his intentions absolutely clear in the autograph score?

5 Gloria

1 The scoring gives us a further clue. During the loud statements of the 'Gloria' motif in Eb (bar 174) and F (bar 210), the trumpets, in D, cannot join in. But even when the music reverts to D and the motif is stated in a playable key (at bar 182), the trumpets do not play the motif but instead hammer the tonic in octaves. The reason for this is to be found in the word-setting: the trumpets help convey the awesome power of God the father ('Pater omnipotens'), preparing the first entry of the trombones in the Mass at bar 185.

2 It is instructive to compare how Haydn came to terms with the same text. In the *Mariazellermesse* (1782) the 'Adoramus te' is subdued; a second 'Laudamus' cycle, with more uniform dynamics for the four phrases, is used to 'cover' the disruption. In the *Theresienmesse* (1799), the 'Laudamus' group is worked out in a similar way.

But in the *Harmoniemesse* (1802), which also has two 'Laudamus' cycles, the 'Adoramus te' in the first is sung quietly in unison while in the second it is omitted altogether! Moreover, Haydn recalls the opening of the Gloria at the first 'Glorificamus te', thus making a musical connection between '*Glori*-a' and '*glori*-ficamus'. To some extent this anticipates Beethoven; the Missa solemnis goes one step further by moving the 'Gloria' recall to the head of the 'Laudamus' group, and introducing a new idea for 'Glorificamus te'.

3 Though the natural notes of the trumpet are the same as those of the horn, the instrument lacks the notes available by hand-stopping. This means that the register of its diatonic scale is much higher than that of the horn, as well as being relatively limited.

In giving the trumpets a Handelian role in this movement, Beethoven is actually moving a step ahead in the field of orchestration – by adding the trumpet to his arsenal of melodic wind instruments – albeit by grafting a Baroque practice onto a late Classical orchestral stock.

4 We perceive these extra statements of 'Miserere nobis', in effect, as a new line of text mainly on account of the radical tonal break between bar 291 (F major) and bar 292 (F♯ minor). The two-phrase structure is clarified by the slight change in the wording of bars 296–305. 'O, miserere nobis' (in the solo parts) and 'ah, miserere nobis' (in the choral parts) are the responses to the simple opening statement of 'miserere nobis'. Without this modification, there would be no distinction between the texts set by the component phrases. Viewed from the other side, the phrase structure justifies Beethoven's unprecedented changes in the text.

5 A similar tension is created in the first movement of the Ninth Symphony, where the trumpets and timpani are again a third too high for the tonality of the second subject group. But it is attenuated there by the more complex bass line: the tonic and dominant chords of Bb are frequently placed in first inversion (bars 102, 106, 122, 133 and 138). In this passage from the Mass, the conflict between structural bass line and orchestration is undiluted, and unambiguous.

  I shall return to this point in the general discussion of orchestration in chapter 9.

6 Compare the finale of the Sonata in A major, op.101, bars 248–51, a movement which, moreover, has strong fugal elements.

6 Credo

1 Mozart's Mass in F major, K.192, also uses a four-note 'Credo' motif as a refrain; it is unlikely, however, that this work could have served as a model for Beethoven.

2 The progression from Bb to Db is the same as that found in the Larghetto of the Gloria, at the second 'miserere nobis' (bar 273). Though I do not believe that the 'Qui propter' was intended, or is easy to hear, as a reference to this passage, the sentiments of the text are comparable, and thus appropriately use the same harmonic materials.

3 Beethoven's unorthodox accentuation of '*des*-cen-dit' (see especially bars 112–15) is based on Classical Latin prosody rather than on the conventional stress patterns observed in medieval liturgical texts; this peculiarity is emphasized in the annotations to his handwritten copy of the Mass text, and is not repeated elsewhere in the Missa solemnis.

4 That Beethoven's modality is derived primarily from nineteenth-century theoretical writings on the subject, and not on his study of authors such as Glarean and Zarlino, has been persuasively argued by Sieghard Brandenburg in a historical study of the 'Heiliger Dank-gesang' (1982).

5 As mentioned in chapter 1, some writers have assigned the 'Et incarnatus' to the Lydian (F) mode, largely on the strength of the persistent B♮s; but the opening fifth d^1–a^1 identifies the principal degrees of the Dorian scale, and these are supported by the harmonies at the ends of the phrases: D in bar 131, A major in bar 142.

6 To find a precedent for this extraordinary passage we must turn to Classical opera: the episode in *Don Giovanni* (Act I, scene 2) in which the Don fatally wounds the Commenda-tore. The duel is fought in D minor; the subsequent trio in F minor, depicting the Commendatore's agony and death, develops unexpectedly from a diminished seventh-chord and is extended beyond its goal by chromatic part-writing: F minor 6–4 chord, C major, C minor, G major sixth-chord. The ensuing dialogue between Don Giovanni and Leporello sounds harmonically irrelevant in its context; it is only when the orchestra enters to express Donna Anna's horror at the sight of her father's corpse ('Ma qual mai s'offre') that the tragic thread of the drama is resumed.

7 Owing to limitations of space, I have summarized my analysis of the fugue in Table 3 and confined my discussion to a few brief remarks. For a fuller discussion of its structure, see Zickenheiner 1984, especially pp. 74–98.

7 Sanctus

1 Beethoven, I believe, failed to understand the implications of returning to the first 'Osanna' in his earlier setting of the Mass. After a broad, highly lyrical Benedictus in Γ, covering 129 bars in a tempo of *allegretto ma non troppo*, the *da capo* of a sixteen-bar 'Osanna', a fugal *allegro* in A, sounds disconcertingly abrupt.

8 Agnus Dei

1 The two-part form does not apply to a *missa brevis*, such as Haydn's Little Organ Mass of around 1775, where the entire movement might be set in one tempo. 'Home key' requires clarification: the 'Dona' was always set in the major, even when the Mass began in the minor (for example, Haydn's 'Nelson' Mass).

2 A significant precedent for the rarely used key of a B minor in symphonic music is the *Trauermarsch* from Beethoven's incidental music to *Leonore Prohaska*, WoO 96 no. 4 (1815), which is his own orchestration, for wind band, of the *Marcia funebre* from the Sonata op.26 (originally in Ab minor).

3 Even in the earliest draft of the 'Agnus', which suggests a simple three-part form, Beethoven marks the agitated middle section 'Krieg, Sturm' ('War, Storm'). In the autograph score, the 'Dona' was originally marked 'darstellend den innern und äußern Frieden' ('representing inner and outer peace'); this was changed to the more titular 'Bitte um innern und äußern Frieden' ('prayer for inner and outer peace').

4 It would be foolish to guess, from the absence of trumpets and timpani before bar 174, that they would enter in a foreign key at some 'dramatic' point in the 'Dona'. As early as 1808, in the 'Pastoral' Symphony, Beethoven took the unprecedented step of scoring a symphonic finale more lightly than one of the interior movements (that is, without piccolo, trumpets or timpani). The addition of instruments in the Mass, like their removal from the Symphony, is for programmatic purposes.

5 Beethoven's own concertos behave differently, placing greater emphasis on striking motifs (in the earlier concertos) or on thematic development (especially in the later ones). His reliance on more Mozartian thematic procedures in the 'Dona' may be further evidence of the Mass's alienated position in music history (see Adorno 1964).

6 The fading-out of the military component of the orchestra – one drum, marked *p – sempre più p – ppp –* is of course Beethoven's way of depicting the end of the War. These drum solos are hinted at by a relatively early remark in the sketches, 'zule[t]zt timpani als Friedenszeichen' ('timpani at the end, as a sign of Peace').

9 Concluding thoughts

1 The composition history, as far as one can make it out from the surviving sketches, supports this picture. The Kyrie and Gloria were essentially in place by the end of 1819, and their relationship (a slow, quiet, relatively short Kyrie as prelude to a loud, animated, complex and massive Gloria) follows early nineteenth-century practice (Haydn, *Harmoniemesse*; Beethoven, Mass in C). The later movements, however, underwent considerable expansion after the March 1820 deadline had passed. Even if it were not possible to guess the size of the Credo fugue from the early jottings for it, the sketches for the 'Benedictus', the 'Agnus' and the 'Dona' all show Beethoven working towards ever larger designs during the last two-and-a-half years of the composition.

Bibliography

Standard reference works and biographies of Beethoven

Anderson 1961   *The Letters of Beethoven*, ed. and trans. Emily Anderson, 3 vols. (London, 1961).

Johnson, Tyson and Winter 1985   Douglas Johnson, Alan Tyson and Robert Winter: *The Beethoven Sketchbooks* (Berkeley, California and Oxford, 1985).

Kerman and Tyson 1983   Joseph Kerman and Alan Tyson: *The New Grove 'Beethoven'* (London, 1983).

Kinsky and Halm 1955; Dorfmüller 1978   George Kinsky and Hans Halm: *Das Werk Beethovens* (Munich, 1955) [the standard Beethoven thematic catalogue]; supplement in *Beiträge zur Beethoven-Bibliographie*, ed. Kurt Dorfmüller (Munich, 1978), pp. 281–440.

Schindler 1966   Anton Felix Schindler: *Beethoven as I Knew Him*, trans. of *Biographie von Ludwig van Beethoven*, revised 3rd ed. (Münster, 1860), Constance S. Jolly, ed. Donald MacArdle (London, 1966).

Schott 1985   *Ludwig van Beethoven: der Briefwechsel mit dem Verlag Schott*, ed. Beethoven-Haus Bonn (Munich, 1985).

Thayer 1967   Alexander Wheelock Thayer: *Thayer's Life of Beethoven*, revised and ed. Elliot Forbes, 2nd ed. (Princeton, 1967).

Life-and-works studies with substantial discussion of the *Missa solemnis*

Bekker 1912   Paul Bekker: *Beethoven* (Berlin and Leipzig, 1912).

Bekker 1925   Paul Bekker: *Beethoven*, trans. M. M. Bozman (London, 1925) [abridged trans. of Bekker 1912].

Cooper 1970   Martin Cooper: *Beethoven: the Last Decade 1817–1827* (London, 1970).

Dahlhaus 1987   Carl Dahlhaus: *Ludwig van Beethoven und seine Zeit* (Laaber, 1987).

Marx 1863   Adolf Bernhard Marx: *Ludwig van Beethoven: Leben und Schaffen*, 2nd ed. (Berlin, 1863).

Mellers 1985   Wilfrid Mellers: *Beethoven and the Voice of God* (London, 1985).

Riezler 1938   Walter Riezler: *Beethoven*, trans. G. D. H. Pidcock (London, 1938).

Solomon 1977   Maynard Solomon: *Beethoven* (New York, 1977).

Studies of the *Missa solemnis*

Adorno 1964 Theodor Adorno: 'Verfremdetes Hauptwerk: zur *Missa Solemnis*' (1959), *Moments musicaux* (Frankfurt am Main, 1964).
   'Alienated Masterpiece: the *Missa solemnis*', trans. Duncan Smith, *Telos* 28 (1976), pp. 113–24 [trans. of Adorno 1964].

Bibliography

Drabkin 1991a   William Drabkin: 'The Agnus Dei of Beethoven's *Missa solemnis*: the Growth of its Form', *Beethoven Studies*, ed. W. Kinderman (Lincoln, Nebraska, 1991).

Fischmann 1970   Nathan Fischmann: 'Die Uraufführung der *Missa solemnis*', *Beiträge zur Musikwissenschaft* 12 (1970), pp. 274–81.

Fiske 1979   Roger Fiske: *Beethoven's Missa Solemnis* (London, 1979).

Georgiades 1977   Thrasybulos G. Georgiades: 'Zu den Satzschlüssen der Missa Solemnis' (1971), *Kleine Schriften* (Tutzing, 1977), pp. 157–65.

Kinderman 1985–6   William Kinderman: 'Beethoven's Symbol for the Deity in the *Missa solemnis* and the Ninth Symphony', *19th Century Music* 9 (1985–6), pp. 102–18.

Kirkendale 1970   Warren Kirkendale: 'New Roads to Old Ideas in Beethoven's *Missa solemnis*', *Musical Quarterly* 56 (1970), pp. 665–701.

'Beethovens *Missa Solemnis* und die rhetorische Tradition', *Beethoven-Symposion Wien 1970*, ed. Erich Schenk (Vienna, 1971), pp. 121–58 [revised version, in German, of Kirkendale 1970].

Lester 1970   Joel Lester: 'Revisions in the Autograph of the *Missa Solemnis Kyrie*', *Journal of the American Musicological Society* 23 (1970), pp. 420–38.

Magnani 1962   Luigi Magnani: 'La genesi dell'idea della *Missa solemnis*', *I quaderni di conversazione di Beethoven* (Milan and Naples, 1962), pp. 91–109.

McCaldin 1971   Denis McCaldin: 'The Choral Music', *The Beethoven Companion*, ed. D. Arnold and N. Fortune (London, 1971), pp. 387–410.

Nottebohm 1887   Gustav Nottebohm: *Zweite Beethoveniana* (Leipzig, 1887) [includes the essays 'Skizzen zur Zweiten Messe', pp. 148–56; 'Drei Skizzenhefte aus den Jahren 1819 bis 1822', pp. 460–75].

Pousseur 1979   Henri Pousseur: 'La *Missa solemnis*, miroir d'un conflit beethovénien', *Schweizerische Musikzeitung* 119 (1979), pp. 18–26.

Schmitz 1963   Arnold Schmitz: 'Zum Verständnis der Gloria in Beethovens Missa solemnis', *Festschrift Friedrich Blume zum 70. Geburtstag*, ed. Anna Amalie Abert and Walter Pfannkuch (Kassel, 1963).

Tovey 1937   Donald F. Tovey: 'Beethoven: *Missa solemnis*, Op.123', *Essays in Musical Analysis* 5 (London, 1937), pp. 161–84.

Virneisel 1966   Wilhelm Virneisel: 'Zur Handschrift der *Missa solemnis* von Beethoven', *Österreichische Musikzeitschrift* 21 (1966), pp. 261–8.

Weber 1908   Wilhelm Weber: *Beethovens Missa solemnis: eine Studie*, 2nd ed. (Leipzig, 1908).

Winter 1984   Robert Winter: 'Reconstructing Riddles: the Sources for Beethoven's *Missa solemnis*', *Beethoven Essays: Studies in Honor of Elliot Forbes*, ed. Lewis Lockwood and Phyllis Benjamin (Cambridge, Mass., 1984), pp. 217–50.

Zickenheiner 1984   Otto Zickenheiner: *Untersuchungen zur Credo-Fuge der Missa solemnis von Ludwig van Beethoven* (Munich, 1984).

Modern editions of the score and of source materials

Schmidt-Görg 1952–70   *Ludwig van Beethoven: Drei Skizzenbücher zur Missa solemnis*, facsimile and transcription, transcribed with notes and commentary by Joseph Schmidt-Görg, 6 vols. (Bonn, 1952–70).

Schmidt-Görg 1970–2   *Ludwig van Beethoven: Ein Skizzenbuch zu den Diabelli-Variationen und zur Missa solemnis*, facsimile and transcription, transcribed with notes and commentary by Joseph Schmidt-Görg, 2 vols. (Bonn, 1970–2); see also Winter 1975.

Hess 1964   *Beethoven: Missa solemnis*, ed. Willy Hess (London, *c.* 1964) [Eulenburg miniature score].

Virneisel 1965   *Ludwig van Beethoven: Missa solemnis, op.123: Kyrie*, facsimile of the autograph score, with an accompanying booklet by Wilhelm Virneisel (Tutzing, 1965).

Bibliography

Related studies

Brandenburg 1982   Sieghard Brandenburg: 'The Historical Background to the "Heiliger Dankgesang" in Beethoven's A-minor Quartet Op.132', *Beethoven Studies 3*, ed. A. Tyson (Cambridge, 1982), pp. 161–91.

Brandenburg 1988   'Die Beethovenhandschriften in der Musikaliensammlung des Erzherzogs Rudolph', *Zu Beethoven, 3: Aufsätze und Dokumente*, ed. H. Goldschmidt (Berlin 1988), pp. 141–76.

Butt 1991   John Butt: *Bach: Mass in B Minor* (Cambridge, 1991).

Churgin 1987   Bathia Churgin: 'Beethoven and Mozart's *Requiem*: a New Source', *Journal of Musicology* 4 (1987), pp. 157–77.

Drabkin 1991b   William Drabkin: 'Beethoven's Understanding of "Sonata Form": the Evidence of the Sketchbooks', *Beethoven Studies*, ed. W. Kinderman (Lincoln, Nebraska, 1991).

Hoffmann 1920   E. T. A. Hoffmann: *Musikalische Novellen und Aufsätze*, ed. E. Istel, vol. 2 (Regensburg, 1920).

Solomon 1982   Maynard Solomon: 'Beethoven's Tagebuch of 1812–1818', *Beethoven Studies 3*, ed. A. Tyson (Cambridge, 1982), pp. 193–288 [also in *Beethoven Essays* (Cambridge, Mass., 1988), pp. 233–95].

Solomon 1983   Maynard Solomon: 'Beethoven: The Quest for Faith', *Beethoven-Jahrbuch* 10 (1983), pp. 101–19 [also in *Beethoven Essays* (Cambridge, Mass., 1988), pp. 216–29].

Webster 1980   James Webster: 'Sonata Form', *The New Grove Dictionary of Music*, ed. S. Sadie (London, 1980), vol. 17, pp. 497–508.

Winter 1975   Robert Winter: review of Schmidt-Görg 1970–2 in *Journal of the American Musicological Society* 28 (1975), pp. 135–8.

Index